MR SMITH'S
FRUIT GARDEN

by Geoffrey Smith

Illustrated by Colin Gray
Edited by Brian Davies

BRITISH BROADCASTING CORPORATION

Published to accompany the BBC-tv series *Mr Smith's Fruit Garden* produced by Peter Riding and Brian Davies and first broadcast on BBC-2 from September to October 1977

Published to accompany a series of programmes prepared in consultation with the BBC Further Education Advisory Council.

Other BBC books by the author
Mr Smith's Gardening Book
Mr Smith's Vegetable Garden
Mr Smith's Flower Garden
Mr Smith Propagates Plants

The photographs front and back covers and page 4 were specially taken by Don McPhee.

© Geoffrey Smith and the British Broadcasting Corporation 1976
First published 1977. Reprinted 1978
Published by the British Broadcasting Corporation, 35 Marylebone High Street, London, W1M 4AA.
Set in 9/10 Ehrhardt 453 Monophoto
Printed in England by Alan Pooley Printing Limited, Tunbridge Wells, Kent.
ISBN: 0 563 16111 6

Contents

Introduction

No gardener finds the season measured more exactly than the fruit grower. In Spring there is the loveliness of pink blossom against the blue and white of a cloud-flecked sky. Enjoyment in this case is tinged with anxiety: a late frost could kill the blossom, destroying in one night the harvest for a whole season.

Summer sees the promise swelling to maturity. Feeding, pruning and spraying are routine tasks attended to while nature's own chemistry turns a tiny vessel inside a flower to succulent ripeness.

In turn the harvest is secured: gooseberries start the season and late apples or pears close the orchard year. Then with the flavour still on the tongue – preparing and planting new ground takes us gently into Spring.

Trays of fruit, stored safe from frost, are a comforting insurance against high prices during Winter, but it is the sense of achievement a successful harvest brings which is the gardener's real reward.

Geoffrey Smith

Preface

Some areas of the British Isles are more favourable to fruit growing than others. Fortunately there are few locations where it is impossible to grow any fruit at all. Even when there is no garden available a patio, balcony, or yard, with effort and ingenuity can be turned into a mini-orchard. The scope is restricted, but strawberries planted in barrels will yield quality fruit as will figs, apples and peaches cultivated in tubs.

All sections of gardening have their own descriptive phrases; fruit is no exception. Two terms frequently used are 'top' and 'soft' fruit. Top fruit as the name implies covers apples, pears, plums, cherries and peaches. Soft or bush fruit is a collective term which includes blackcurrants, raspberries and gooseberries.

Apart from raspberries and strawberries which come into crop 18 months after planting, fruit growing is a long-term project. So to save time and effort draw up a plan.

Fruit can be an ornamental feature, so instead of growing crab apples in the flower beds, choose a dessert variety which will, in due course, provide edible fruit. Walls can be used to support specially trained apples, pears or cherries.

DO NOT be tempted to plant more trees or bushes than the available space will comfortably hold. Overcrowding will lead to all sorts of problems and in the competition for light, the trees are weakened and become susceptible to attack from pests and diseases.

Try to make certain there is shelter from cold winds which prevent pollinating insects visiting the flowers; without adequate pollination no fruit will develop. Low-lying gardens can be so sheltered they become frost pockets; cold air, like water, gathers at the lowest point, building up until it covers the trees killing the blossom.

Strawberries are best grown in the vegetable garden, as every third year they need a change of site, and a well-cultivated soil provides fertile conditions.

The varieties of fruit grown in gardens will not breed true from seed, so must be propagated by budding, grafting, cuttings or runners, which is what the term 'vegetative' propagation means. Any of these methods, unlike growing from seed, will give young plants identical in every respect to the parent variety.

TOOLS

Apart from the tools usually included in a basic gardening kit, spade, hoe and rake, some specialist equipment will be necessary.

A pair of *secateurs* – choose the strongest which can be comfortably handled – a half-inch thick apple or pear branch is a tough proposition.

A *pruning saw* with a narrow blade enables unwanted branches to be cut out close to the main stem.

A *sprayer* to help with pest and disease control.

Soil Preparation

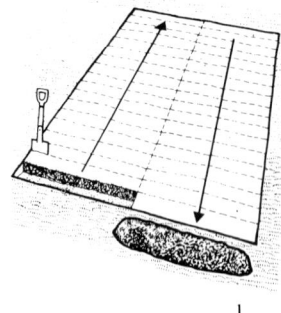

1

Before planting either top or soft fruit, dig the soil over thoroughly. Even when trees are grown in a lawn or paddock the holes to receive them must be well prepared. Take out the soil 18 inches deep and mix it with well-rotted manure and a dressing of general fertilizer. Small areas can be double dug with a spade, removing any weeds at the same time. Weeds look unsightly and they deprive the fruit of water and food. Pay particular attention to removing persistent, perennial weeds like couch, docks or creeping buttercup, which are hard to get rid of once the fruit crop is planted.

Divide the bed down the centre into two equal parts. Take out a trench 16–18 inches wide to the full depth of a spade across the end of one half of the bed (1).

Leave the soil in a heap at the same end of the bed but opposite the untouched half section, where it will be conveniently placed to fill up the trench left when the digging of both sections is completed.

2

Spread compost or manure in the trench (2) then dig this in, working the soil the full depth of the fork prongs along the trench bottom. Mark off the next strip then dig this over with a spade inverting the soil over the forked-up portion of the first trench. Make sure the newly opened up trench is a full spade depth before sprinkling on the compost and forking it in. Repeat the whole sequence down one side of the plot then up the other. When the work is done the plot will be composted and in a loose well-aired condition to a depth of 15–18 inches. Allow the soil to weather and settle for a month or two, then check to see if a dressing of lime is required. Though the majority of fruit crops will grow well in an acid soil, this must not be extreme. The acidity or alkalinity of a soil is expressed by the symbol pH and a number. The term pH7 indicates the soil is neutral, anything below that shows an increasingly acid soil, anything above is one that is progressively richer in free lime. A small kit by which the test is made can be bought cheaply from horticultural suppliers. Should the colour of the mixture in the test tube, when compared with the colour chart supplied with the kit, show a reading below 5.5 pH, give the bed a dressing of lime. DO NOT over lime, as this can cause a shortage of essential minerals, for example iron

3

Thorough preparation of the soil by hand on a small scale is a practical suggestion, but on any area larger than the average (10 × 30 yards) time will be saved by hiring a mechanical cultivator (3). A small plough will bury the weed in autumn; leave the surface to weather then a month before planting, work in the well-rotted compost with a rotovator. On heavy land DO NOT use a rotovator when the soil is wet, because it can cause damage to the structure so that drainage from the surface becomes poor and water gathers in pools after every shower of rain. The soil should be kept cleanly cultivated for the first two or three years until the trees are established and then sown down to grass for easy maintenance. This grassing down will also slow down the trees' rate of growth and bring them into fruit bearing. The feeding programme is adjusted accordingly if the growth becomes too stunted.

The rate at which various fertilizers are applied differs between soils and is influenced by the condition of the trees. Already established fruit trees should be mulched with well-rotted manure in early Spring and those growing in grassland in late Spring, if necessary.

Shortage of nitrogen shows in poor, weak growth. Phosphorus deficiency is indicated in poor growth, lack of flowers and bitter fruit. Potash is essential to balanced growth and any shortage shows in the leaves which scorch at the edges, and in extreme cases the fruit is shed while still immature (not to be confused with June drop – a natural annual occurrence). Mulching with compost or rotted manure plus a dressing of fertilizer compound will correct this. A shortage of nitrogen can be corrected by spraying the leaves with a foliar feed.

On light or very limey soils fruit trees may show a yellowing between the veins, one of the signs that the tree is short of magnesium. In severe cases the leaves fall early and the fruit stops swelling. To correct the condition spray the foliage once a month for 3 months with a solution of 2 teaspoonfuls of Epsom salts (magnesium sulphate) to a gallon of water, commencing in Spring immediately the blossom fades.

Iron deficiency is a fairly common condition on soils which contain a heavy concentration of lime. Tips of the young growing shoots turn yellow and the branch may die back, particularly the young spurs. As with magnesium shortage, this can be corrected by spraying the foliage with Sequestrene or similar soluble iron chelates. Soil applications of iron should be made during the Winter as the material is absorbed slowly compared to foliage sprays, and takes several months to have an effect.

Weed control, especially close to the trees where mechanical cultivators could cause root damage, may be done with one of the modern herbicides. Any weed killer must be used with care or it may kill more than the weeds!

KEEP ALL POISONOUS MATERIAL IN A LOCKED CUPBOARD AWAY FROM CHILDREN.

'Paraquat' kills only through green tissue – leaves, buds or shoots, so in addition to controlling weeds it is a help in killing unwanted sucker growths between raspberry rows and on top fruit.

Dichlobenil may be used around trees or bushes which have been planted 2 years and are established. The chemical persists in the soil for anything up to 6 months, unlike 'Paraquat' which breaks down on contact with the soil.

NEVER use any chemicals for pest, disease or weed control carelessly. READ the instructions carefully and follow them exactly.

Thoroughly WASH hands, if necessary clothes, and spray equipment once the spraying is finished.

In the small fruit garden weed control is best done by hand – the purchase of chemicals and equipment is a needless expense.

Tree Types

Fruit trees can be trained into various forms, some of them are particularly suitable for growing in a small garden.

Bush trees (1) are the cheapest to buy and easiest to maintain. The main stem is between 18 and 30 inches high with the branches growing out to form a balanced head (branch system). All the top fruit can be grown as bush trees with the possible exception of plums whose branches tend to weep naturally, and so need a longer stem to keep them clear of the ground.

Half standards (2) are trees grown on 3 or 4 feet stems before branches are allowed to develop. Because they are usually grafted onto a vigorous rootstock, they grow large and are not suitable for commercial orchard work.

Standards (3) have even longer stems – up to 6 feet before a branch system is built up, so in maturity make very large trees suitable only for commercial orchard work.

Dwarf pyramids (4) in maturity only grow 7–8 feet high so they are very suitable for the small garden. They are trained so the branch system develops in tiers all round the stem from soil level, gradually getting shorter as they near the top, to produce the pyramid shape which gives the name to this type of tree.

Spindle bush (5) is a tree form which produces a very heavy crop while occupying only a small amount of space. To maintain the cone shape, pull down the lowest branches almost horizontally, while the top are treated as fruiting spurs and cut back hard each year. A good strong post is used as a support. As the branches are pulled down under the weight of crop, use strings tied to the top of the post to support them. To maintain a spindle bush in full cropping order needs time and understanding of the pruning required.

Cordons (6) consist of a single straight stem on which side growths are restricted by pruning to form fruit spurs. No branches are allowed to grow, which means regular pruning from early Summer onwards. Because growth is narrow and upright, a lot of trees can be accommodated in a very small garden.

Espalier (7) A tree grown on an espalier consists of a main stem from which more or less opposite pairs of branches are trained out at right angles on each side. This method is used mainly for apples and pears which are tolerant of hard pruning.

Fan training (8) as the name implies, is a system of directing branches outwards from a short central stem in precisely the same manner as the ribs of an open fan.

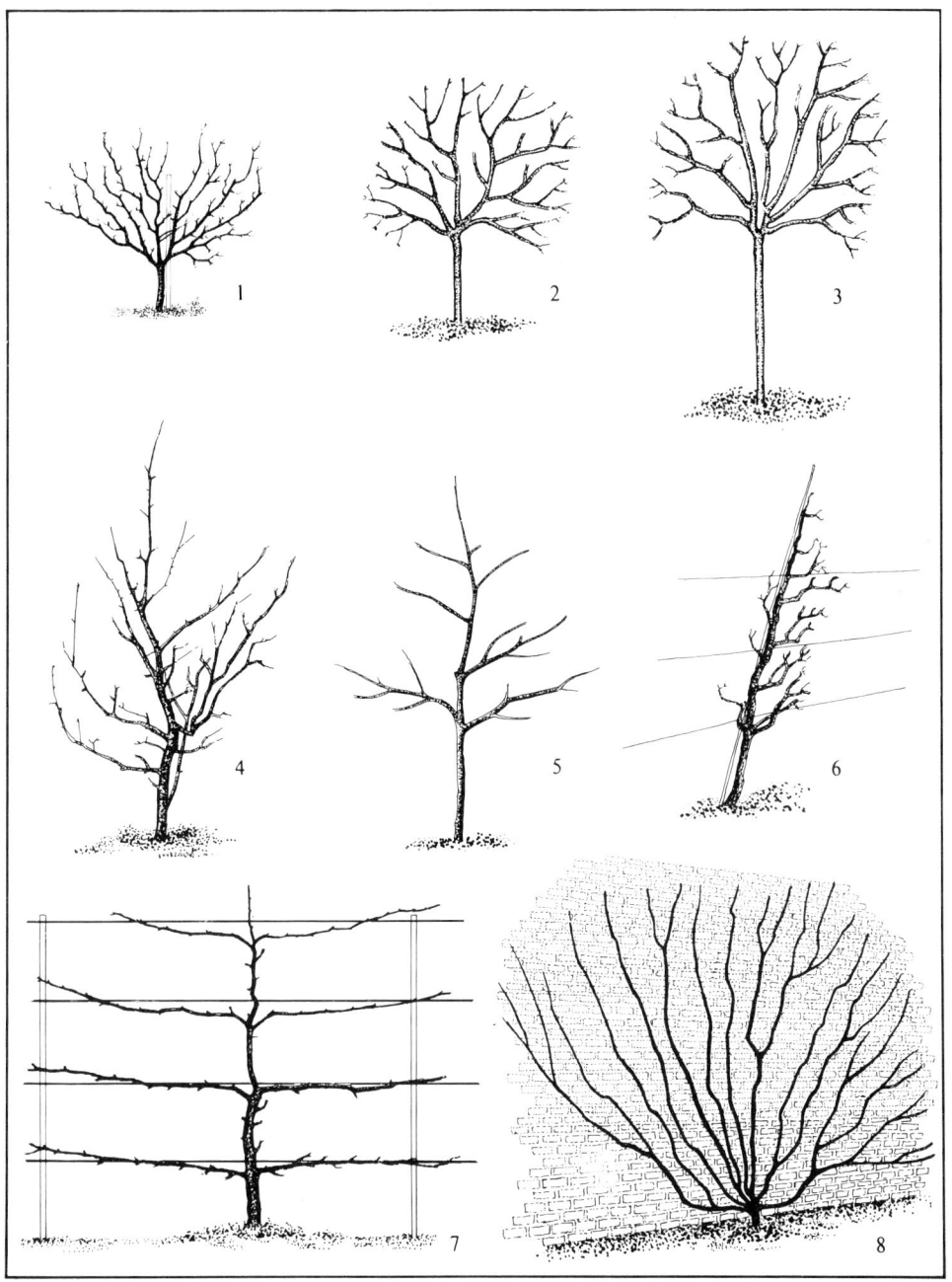

1

2

3

4

5

6

7

8

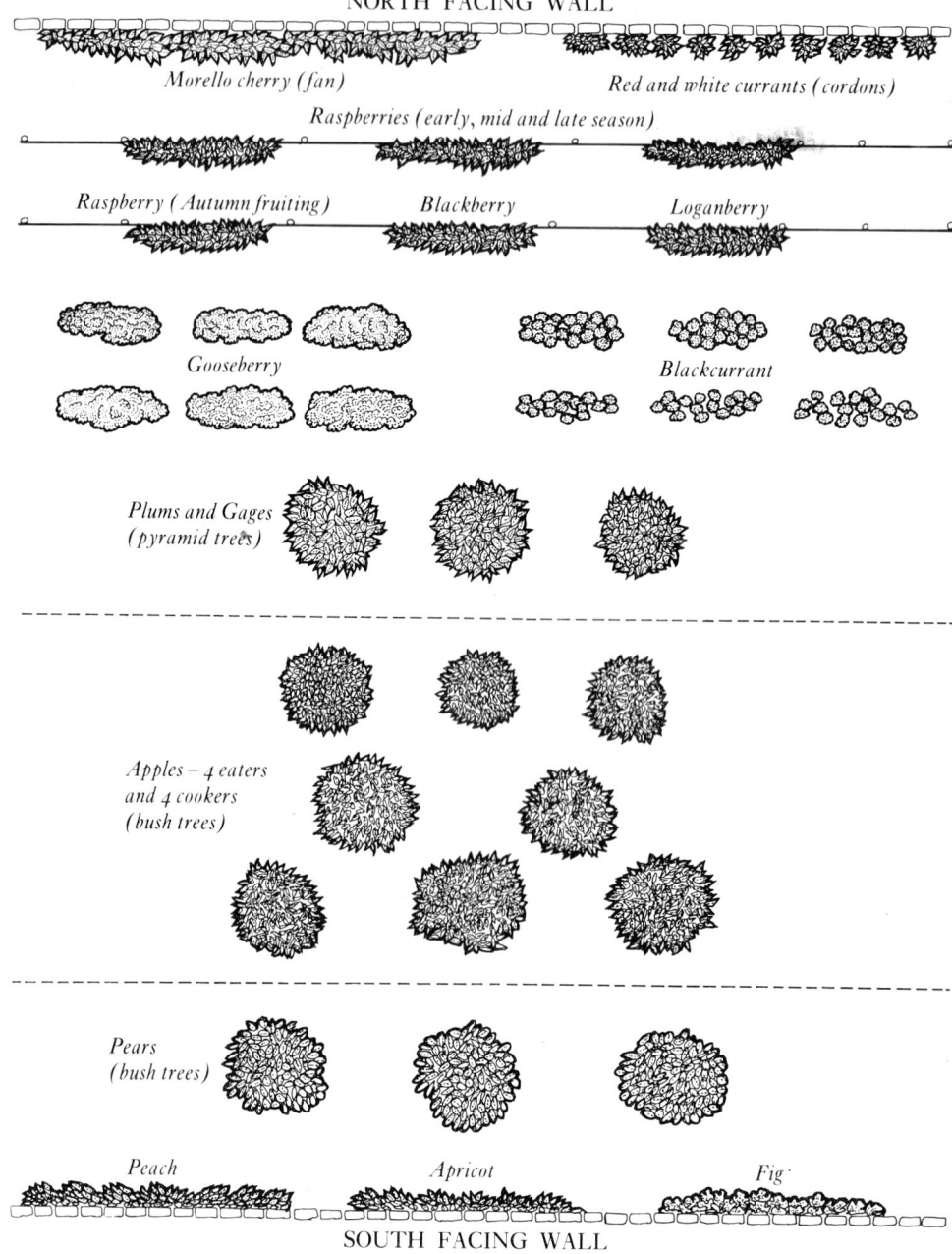

NORTH FACING WALL

Morello cherry (fan)   Red and white currants (cordons)

Raspberries (early, mid and late season)

Raspberry (Autumn fruiting)   Blackberry   Loganberry

Gooseberry   Blackcurrant

Plums and Gages
(pyramid trees)

Apples – 4 eaters
and 4 cookers
(bush trees)

Pears
(bush trees)

Peach   Apricot   Fig

SOUTH FACING WALL

Only a proportion of the available space in a garden can be devoted to fruit growing. The plan is based on a plot size 30 × 90 feet.

The Morello cherries, red and white currants, will crop on a north-facing wall or fence. No provision is made for growing sweet cherries which are difficult to manage in a small garden. Morello cherries are grown fan trained and so can be netted to prevent bird damage. Grow the currants as triple cordons on the wall or fence.

Raspberries will be partially shaded, 10 feet of row devoted to each variety: 'Malling Jewel', 'Glen Cora', 'Malling Admiral' or 'Norfolk Giant'. A 10 feet run of raspberry 'Zeva' or 'September' would provide fruit in late Summer and Autumn.

Blackberries and loganberries require much the same soil conditions and 8–10 feet of growing space each.

Because cordons require considerable attention to pruning during the Summer, only the devoted fruit grower will attempt their cultivation. Four rows of cordon apples would fit in the space allocated to 8 bush apples. Spindle and dwarf pyramid trees need slightly less attention, bush forms the least of all.

In a garden of this size, whatever the form chosen, the trees should be worked onto a dwarfing root stock. Then in maturity they will take up no more than the space allowed and the routine work of pruning, spraying and picking will be very much easier to do. In most fruit growing areas birds are a pest, destroying blossom buds before they open. Trees on a dwarfing stock can be given some protection against this type of damage by netting, cottoning or spraying.

Choice of varieties depends on personal preference. The majority should be of those which keep well in store, so a succession of good quality fruit is available throughout the Winter and Spring.

Pears are easier to manage when grown as bush trees, but they will crop well as cordons or dwarf pyramids. Unlike apples they do not store well, so 3 trees should be enough.

Peaches and apricots will ripen outdoors even in northern areas, given the shelter of a south facing wall. Figs need the protection of a greenhouse in all except the most favoured areas. The trees are easier to prune if grown fan trained.

Gooseberries are the most reliable fruit, succeeding over a wide range of soils and exposed situations. Choose varieties with green, red and yellow berries, leaving some on each bush to ripen for dessert. Six bushes will give enough fruit for a family of four with plenty to spare. Birds can be a problem, stripping the buds in late Winter.

The 6 blackcurrants well mulched will crop well enough to keep up a succession of pies almost the whole year round if stored in a deep freeze, and leave enough for jam making.

In a small garden choose the most economical fruit: gooseberries, strawberries, raspberries, blackcurrants and apples.

Planting

1

Planting may be carried out at any time during the dormant season (when the tree or shrub has no leaves), MID-OCTOBER to MARCH.

NEVER PLANT when the soil is very wet or frozen.

When the trees arrive from the nursery unpack them, and if the roots are dry, stand them in a tank of water to soak for $1\frac{1}{2}$–2 hours. If the plants cannot be put in their permanent positions immediately, dig a hole, lay the roots onto it, cover them with soil, topped off with a layer of straw if the weather turns frosty. When weather and soil conditions are suitable, the trees or bushes can be planted directly into their permanent places.

Take out a hole large enough to accommodate the roots properly. The union between the rootstock and shoot of the variety grafted on it, which shows as a swelling on the stem, should be 3–4 inches above soil level, so do not make the hole too deep (1). Replace the soil a little at a time, working it between the fine roots with the fingers and firming gently with the feet.

Both half standard and standard trees should be staked when planted. Place a stout stake in such a position that when the tree stem is tied it will be given maximum support without the risk of chafing. Secure the tree firmly to the stake with one of the proprietory straps which are designed so that there is no danger of damage through the tie becoming too tight (2).

RULES OF PLANTING

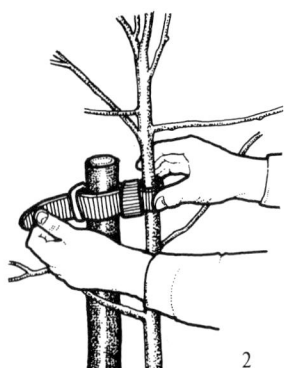

2

Make the hole large enough but not too deep.

Trim any damaged or diseased roots away before planting.

Firm the soil well but do not over compact.

Make sure staking is adequate enough to prevent wind rock.

When fan, espalier or cordon trees are to be grown against a wall remember that the soil at the base may be permanently dry and poor. To ensure the trees get the best possible start, step the roots out from the wall to a distance of 10–12 inches. Excavate the existing soil and replace it with loam from the vegetable garden. To make certain this is in good fertile condition mix in peat, well-rotted manure or compost. The fertility and water–holding potential of the soil, once the trees are planted, is maintained by mulching and by feeding with fertilizer.

Where there is no wall space available, cordons or espalier may be grown on supports formed by wires stretched between strong posts. There should be 6–7 feet of post showing above soil level. Space the posts 10–12 feet apart and stretch wires between them 2 feet apart. Cordons can be trained onto canes set at an angle on the wires.

When training espaliers, pull the branches down slowly into position to avoid breaking them. Tie canes at an angle across from the main stem. Fasten the side branches onto the canes, which can be lowered gradually onto the wires to reduce the risk of damage.

Apples

CULTIVATION

The most popular of the top fruits which, if the right variety is chosen, will succeed in most parts of the British Isles. When choosing young trees it is important to know which rootstock they are grafted on to, because this will influence how big the mature tree will be and at what age it will come into crop. When choosing a rootstock you must take into account the size of the garden and the type of soil. A rootstock which would produce an enormous tree on good soil would grow with considerably less vigour on poor light land. When in doubt about the vigour of the stock or quality of your soil consult a local expert or the nurseryman who is supplying the trees.

Rootstocks M9 and MM106 will produce a dwarf tree. M26 and M7 will give a slightly taller tree which takes a year or two longer on some soils to grow into full crop. For poor soils or where there is sufficient space to hold them, trees on M2 or MM111 will make strong well furnished trees.

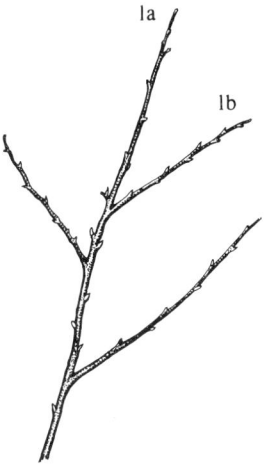

Most nurserymen describe the trees offered for sale as dwarf, medium, or tall, without quoting rootstock numbers at all, which in fact gives all the information required. It is better to ask before you buy.

The enthusiastic amateur who is prepared to take time and trouble in training should buy 1-year-old trees, or maidens. Most nurserymen, however, sell 2- or 3-year-old trees with the head or framework of branches partially formed. Espalier or fans are usually at least 3 years old, which makes them quite expensive. Planting distance depends on the sort of rootstock used and to some extent the variety of apple grafted onto it. Bush trees grown on a less vigorous stock will need spacing 8 feet apart. Cordons grown on the same stock 30 inches, espaliers 10 feet and fan 15 feet. Be generous when in doubt about space. Pruning, to some extent, restricts growth to the available space, but reduces the crop considerably.

Staking and planting of young apple trees is described in detail on the opposite page.

Pruning is essential during the first 3 or 4 years; it is adjusted to form a tree with a strong, well-spaced framework of branches. In subsequent years, pruning is aimed at maintaining the tree in good health and maximum cropping. Again, certain terms are used which need explanation.

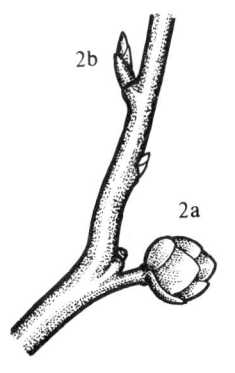

LEADER (1a) is the shoot at the tip of a branch.

LATERAL (1b) is a shoot on the side of a branch.

FRUIT BUDS (2a) differ from growth buds in that they are rounded and plump.

GROWTH BUDS (2b) are slender and less pronounced than fruit buds. They are carried almost flat on the stem. An ability to tell the difference between the two can be acquired by looking carefully at a mature apple tree.

Apples (continued)

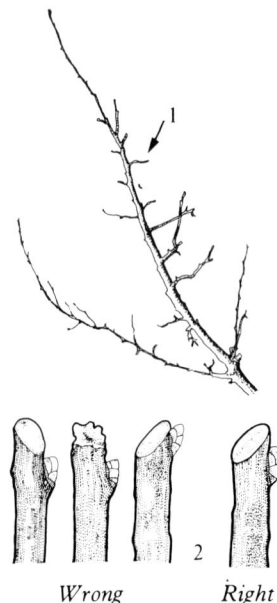

Some apples carry fruit on short sturdy growths which are described as *spurs* (1) – Cox's Orange Pippin is a good example of a spur fruiting apple. Worcester Pearmain and several other popular varieties develop fruit buds on shoots grown the previous Summer, and they are known as tip bearers. So it is an advantage to know the name of each variety as well as to recognise fruit and growth buds.

When pruning make sure the tools used are sharp – saw, secateurs, and knife. Seal all the large wounds with an antiseptic, waterproof compound as a protection against the weather or disease infection. All cuts should be made close to and slanting downwards from a bud (2). DO NOT leave 'snags' to die back above a bud, or anywhere on a tree.

In the first year after planting a tree should only be allowed to bear 1 or 2 fruits for identification purposes, to check if it is the variety ordered. During the first Winter after planting, cut each leader (shoot at the branch tip) back by two-thirds. Select an upward facing bud to cut back to, so that growth the following year will be up and out, keeping the centre of the bush fully open (3).

To keep the growth open from the centre of the tree, rub out any badly placed shoots which develop the following Spring. In the second Winter prune the leaders to continue upward and outward growth. Laterals (side branches) will also have developed: select the most suitable to form the tree's main branch framework and prune them back by half or two-thirds if growth is weak (4). All other laterals should be cut hard back to about 3 buds from the base.

Each pruning season continue to leader prune until the tree form is established, whether the apple being cultivated is a tip or a spur fruiting variety.

Tip bearing varieties do not need heavy pruning. Any shoots not showing fruit buds at the tip are cut hard back to 3 or 4 buds from the base. Shoots carrying fruit buds are left untouched, providing they are not crossing or overcrowded. Cut any surplus shoots away at the base.

Spur bearers are pruned so that old worn-out fruiting spears are cut away to be replaced by vigorous, healthy young shoots which take over the cropping. A young shoot on a spur bearing tree produces growth the first year, fruit buds the next, and crops in the third. Experience will enable the amateur fruit grower to achieve the right balance between growth and fruitfulness. Selected 3-year-old shoots are cut back to the lowest fruit spur; this makes way for young growth. The next Winter the young growths are spaced out and the following Spring each one produces fresh young shoots from the tip, fruit buds lower down. In the third year they fruit and are headed back to form spurs.

Pruning is not complicated provided the person carrying out the work knows what the tree needs by way of shaping in the early years, then once established, how routine maintenance gives heaviest crops. If in doubt about cutting out a branch, think twice and leave it unpruned.

Wrong   *Right*

Cordons are Summer pruned. The shoots grown during the Summer are cut back in AUGUST to within 3 buds of the base. The growths from fruiting spurs are cut back even harder to 1 leaf from the base (1). Leaders on cordons' main stems are NOT pruned unless damaged in some way.

When an apple tree sets a very heavy crop, some of the fruit may have to be thinned, enabling those which are left to reach full size. The centre or crown fruit should be removed first with a sharp knife or pair of scissors, plus any badly placed or misshapen apples, in early JUNE. Later in the month some of the crop will fall from the tree naturally in what is termed the June drop. How much fruit is left to ripen depends on the vigour of the tree and the fertility of the soil. Two apples per truss is a useful guide if the tree is growing well in moist, fertile soil.

1

FEEDING

Organic matter in the form of well-rotted manure, compost etc. spread on the surface of the soil as a mulch (keep it clear of the tree trunk) will conserve moisture and maintain fertility. A dressing of fertilizer each year at 2–3 oz per square yard should supply the food which a tree in full crop needs. The amount of fertilizer applied to the soil can be increased or decreased according to a particular tree's requirements.

Fruit trees, like most other garden crops, need water in dry weather. Manuring, feeding and watering regularly will keep the tree in healthy growth.

When shoot growth is weak and the leaves are small and pale green it indicates starvation. This is caused by allowing grass to grow around young trees before they are well enough established to stand the competition. To reduce the risk of starvation when grassing down young orchards, add extra nitrogen to the feed. A liquid feed of nitrogen over the foliage during the growing season will restore the balance.

Coarse, luxuriant foliage indicates the soil is too well supplied with nitrogen and this can be corrected with extra potash: $1-1\frac{1}{2}$ oz per square yard will be enough in the Spring. Grass helps to take up surplus nitrogen if the trees are growing in a clean, cultivated garden.

Fertilizer should be applied only after studying the tree. See how it is growing and adjust the quantities of nitrogen, phosphates or potash accordingly.

When the soil around the trees is being kept clean cultivated, take care that the roots do not suffer excess damage for this will cause sucker growth. These suckers or young shoots which spring from below the graft are useless and must be removed, either by pulling them away as close to the roots as possible or watering them with a weed killer such as 'Paraquat' which reduces the sucker growth without harming the parent tree. Suckering will largely be avoided if the roots are left undamaged.

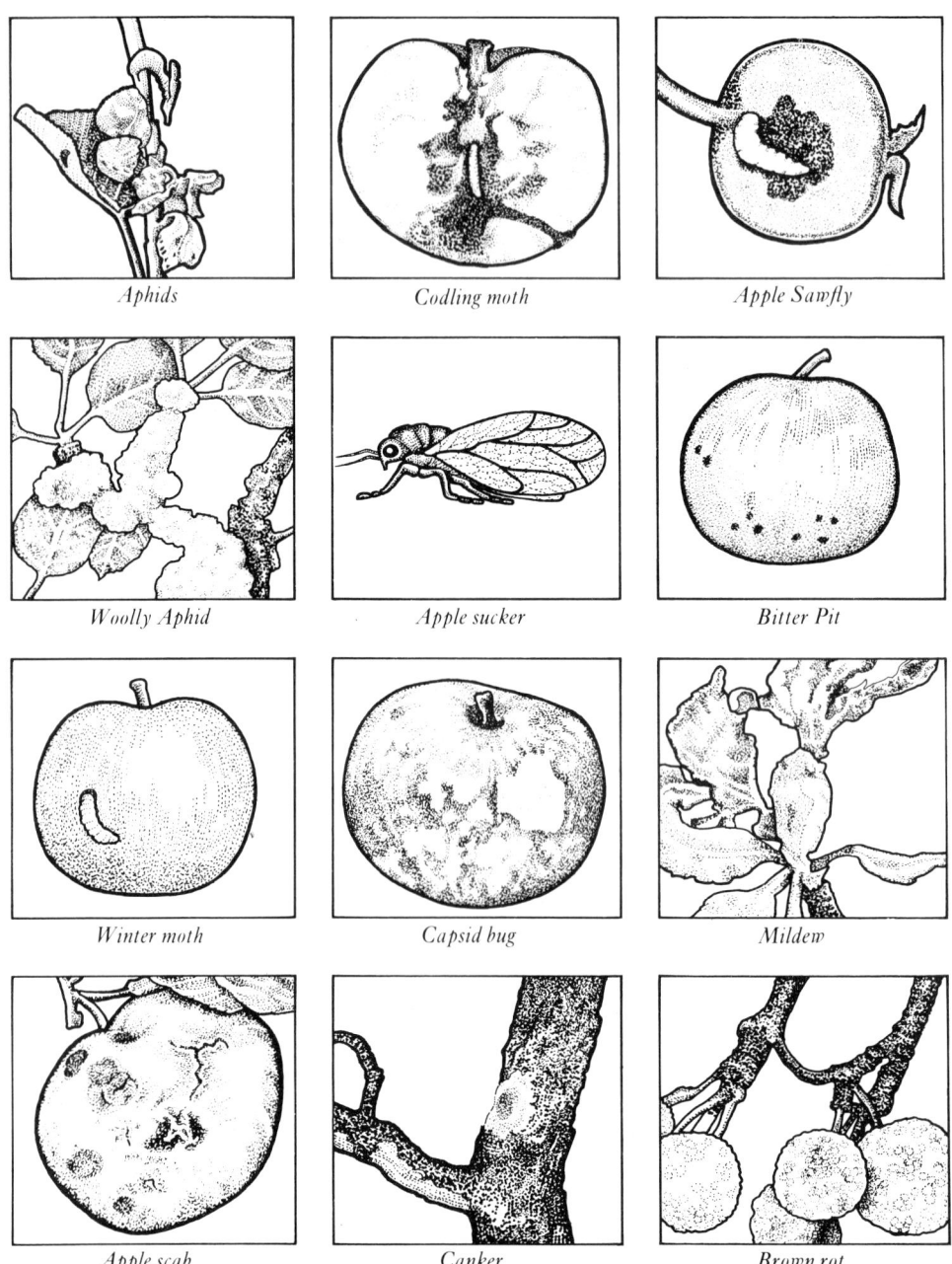

Aphids

Codling moth

Apple Sawfly

Woolly Aphid

Apple sucker

Bitter Pit

Winter moth

Capsid bug

Mildew

Apple scab

Canker

Brown rot

PESTS AND DISEASES

Spraying should be done immediately a pest or disease makes an appearance. Never delay until they reach epidemic proportions.

Aphids (greenfly), which by feeding on the young shoots and foliage seriously weaken the tree, are a major pest. Spray with tar oil wash to kill overwintering eggs. Watch out for the leaves at the shoot tip starting to curl – the first symptoms of attack. Spray with malathion. DO NOT SPRAY WHEN TREES ARE IN BLOOM. Bees and other useful insects may be killed.

Codling moth lays its eggs on the leaves of apple trees in JUNE and the caterpillars which hatch out then burrow into and ruin the fruit. Symptoms are small holes in fruit. Spray with malathion in JUNE and again 3 weeks later to kill caterpillars before they get into the fruit. Caterpillars overwinter under corrugated paper or sacking tied round the tree branches – then they can be collected and destroyed.

Apple Sawfly caterpillars tunnel into young fruits. Spray with malathion immediately the blossom fades. Pick and destroy infested fruits, including those which have fallen to the ground.

Woolly Aphid – like white cotton wool stuck on the branches. Paint the colonies with a brush dipped in malathion or formothion. Spray thoroughly with tar oil or Winter wash.

Apple suckers feed in the young developing flower buds which turn brown. A spray with malathion will give a control.

Bitter Pit affects the fruits and shows itself as sunken pits on the surface of the skin which are surrounded by brown areas. Mulch well and sterilize with 20% formothion.

Winter moth caterpillars feed on the young leaves just as they open and can do a lot of harm. The wingless females climb up from the soil to lay their eggs and can be trapped by bands covered in vegetable grease tied round the stems in later Summer.

Capsid bugs damage the young fruit and leaves by feeding on them. Spray with malathion before and after flowering.

Mildew is a disease which coats leaves and stems with a white floury deposit. Cut out and burn badly infected shoots. Spray with benomyl or dinocap from the pink bud stage at 14-day intervals until JULY.

Apple scab causes the unsightly scab like olive brown blisters on leaves and fruit. Cracks may also develop on the fruit as it swells. Spray with captan, lime sulphur or benomyl from bud burst to JULY at 14-day intervals. Lime sulphur may cause leaf scorch in some varieties, so check instructions before use.

Canker causes sunken patches and die back on young shoots. Cut away diseased tissue and paint the wounds with canker paint.

Brown rot is a fungus which causes rotting of the fruits. The disease infects damaged fruits on the tree and in store. Remove and burn infected fruit to control the spread of the disease.

Apples (continued)

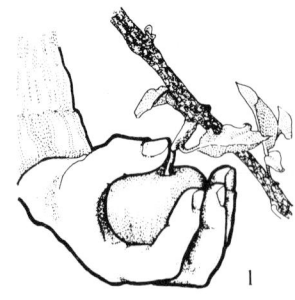

POLLINATION

Almost all varieties of apple will yield a heavier crop if provision is made for cross pollination. This simply means growing more than one variety – choosing those which flower at more or less the same time so that the pollinating insects can effect the interchange of pollen.

There are varieties known as triploids which are not good pollinators, for example Bramley's Seedling, so they must be grown with two other diploid (good pollinators) varieties which flower at the same time to make sure of a good crop. The 2 diploid varieties cross pollinate with the Bramley and each other.

Choose a sheltered position to grow apples so that the cold winds will not prevent pollinating insects from doing their work.

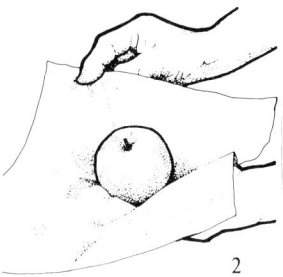

Suitable groupings are possible in a very limited area so long as the trees are grafted onto a dwarfing rootstock, grown as cordons, dwarf pyramids or similar restricted form.

If there is space for only one, then grow a family tree. This is a rootstock on which has been grafted 2 or 3 varieties, all of which require the same treatment in regard to feeding and pruning. Family trees are grafted onto a moderately vigorous rootstock as they need a strong branch system to crop well.

HARVESTING

To test if an apple is ready for picking, lift it in the palm of the hand, then twist (1). If the fruit is ripe, the stalk will part easily from the tree. Handle apples for storage with extreme care, putting to one side for immediate use any which are blemished or damaged in any way. After picking, spread them out on newspapers to sweat for 3 or 4 days before wrapping them in oiled paper or pieces of newspaper (2). Then store in wooden trays (3).

Alternatively, store in polythene bags specially made for the purpose with ventilation holes.

Early varieties are best eaten straight from the tree as they will not keep for long. All apples keep best in a humid atmosphere at a temperature of 40°F. Keep the varieties separate so each one can be removed from the store when ripe enough for use.

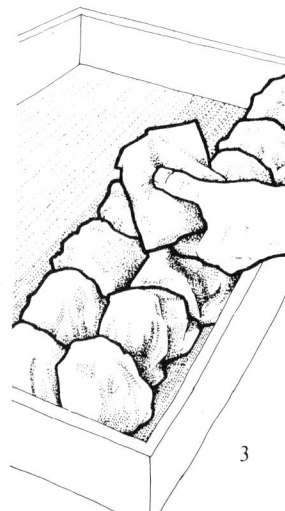

RECOMMENDED VARIETIES (according to season of use).

Dessert Apples
Earlies: 'Discovery', 'Worcester Pearmain'.
Mid-season: 'James Grieve' (rather acid but good pollinator).
Late: 'Sunset', 'Cox's Orange Pippin', 'Golden Delicious'.

Cooking Apples
'Grenadier', 'Warner's King', 'Lane's Prince Albert', 'Monarch', 'Bramley's Seeding'.

Apricots

CULTIVATION

Apricots can be grown outdoors in most areas of the British Isles if situated on a South-facing wall. A fan trained tree is the most suitable for this purpose (1). In mild areas bush trees will crop well but are extremely difficult to protect against bird damage.

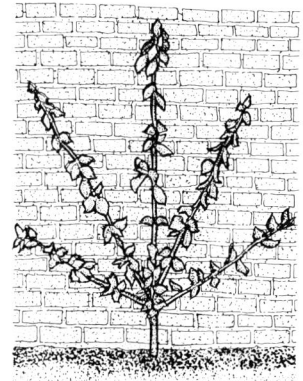

Apricots flower early in the year usually in MARCH to APRIL and are self fertile. So all the gardener has to do is to go over the flowers, transferring the pollen with a piece of dry cotton wool or dried rabbit's tail on a cane. When the weather is mild, insects will do this pollination.

A well-drained soil is essential for growing apricots successfully. Make certain the site, especially for wall planting, is well prepared with rotted manure or compost. If the existing soil is dry and arid, remove it completely. Replace it with a mixture of good chopped loam or cultivated garden soil with compost or well-rotted manure. A little old mortar rubble and lime chippings forked into the bottom of the hole ensures good drainage and provides whatever lime is needed on any but the most acid of soils. DO NOT over-lime as this can cause a mineral deficiency. Mulch with compost or well-rotted manure.

Prune fan trained trees quite hard until the framework is established and there are enough ribs to fill the wall space. Prune in early Spring at this training stage. After pruning apply a complete fertilizer dressing at the rate of 3 oz per square yard. Water the dressing in, do not fork the soil as this could damage the roots. Trees fruit on young shoots of the previous season and old wood. Cut out all badly placed shoots – those growing directly out from or into the wall. Pinch back shoots to half, then after the crop has been picked they should be further reduced to 3 or 4 buds. Complete pruning of established trees before the Autumn.

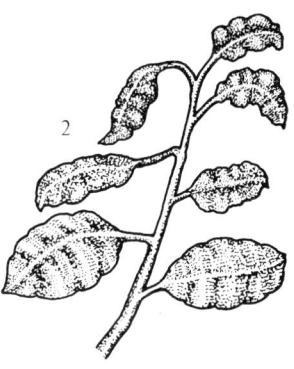

Apricots are ripe when they part easily from the spur and are delicious when eaten sun warmed from the tree.

PESTS AND DISEASES

Leaf curling aphis: these feed on the young shoots and leaves causing stunting and distortion (2). Spray with dimethotate immediately after flowering.

Silver leaf (3): causes young twigs to die back and gives a silvery sheen to the leaves. Cut out all infected branches and paint wounds with Stockholm tar. Make sure the trees are kept fed and watered.

Bacterial canker: die back of smaller branches, holes in the leaves. Cut out infected wood and paint wounds with canker paste. A spray with Bordeaux mixture after pruning will give some protection.

RECOMMENDED VARIETIES

'Moorpark' and 'Hemskerke' are fine flavoured apricots which crop well, given a South wall.

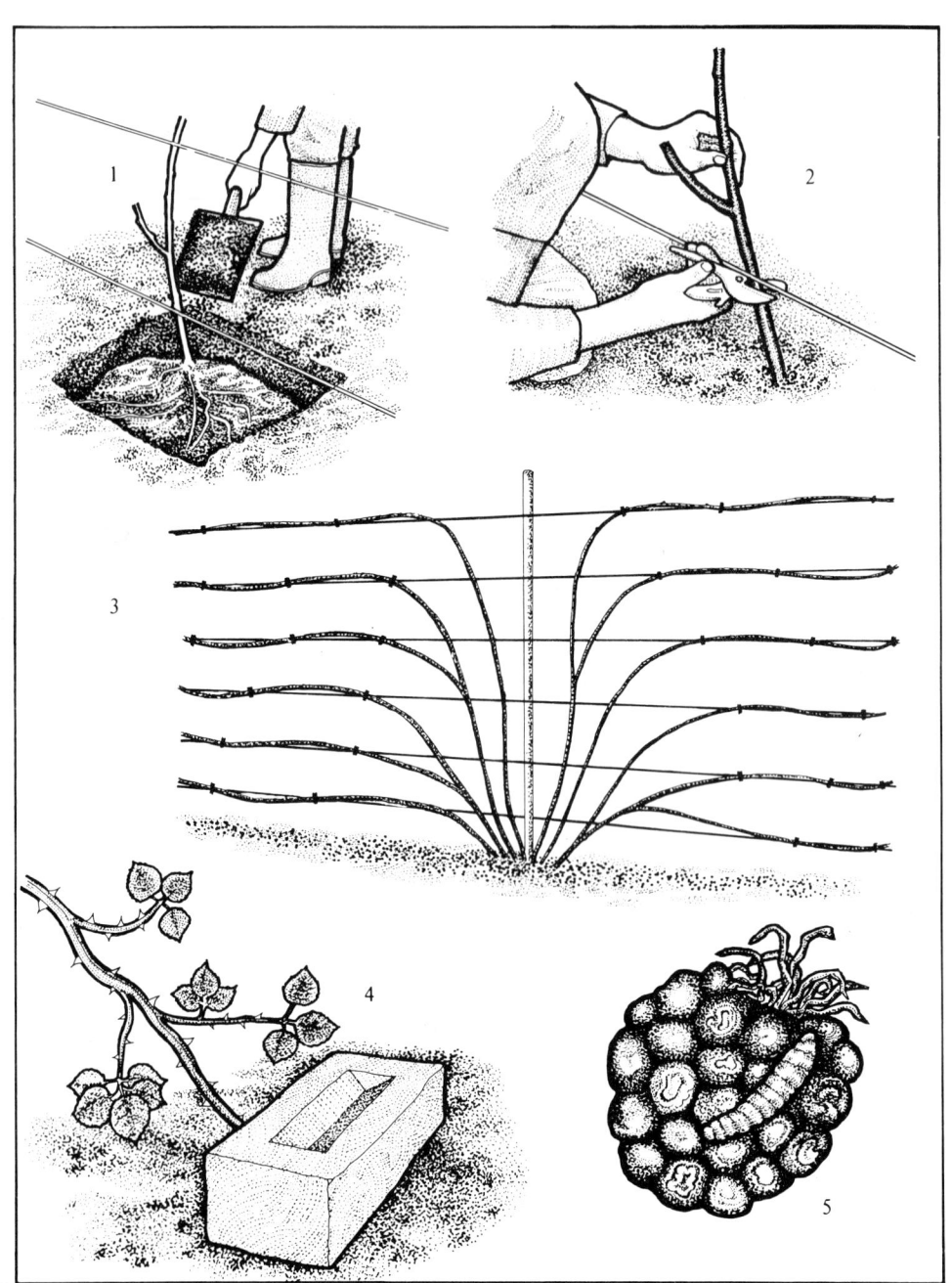

CULTIVATION

Blackberries are easy to grow in almost all soils, but where space is limited choose a less vigorous variety. As they are self fertile and will set a good crop without cross pollination, single bushes can be planted but may not provide enough fruit at any one time for a large family.

A position in full sun is the best, particularly in northern areas, as it produces better flavoured berries.

Dig the soil over, clearing it of perennial weeds; make sure the sub-soil is well broken up to provide good drainage necessary for healthy root growth. Work in leaf mould, or compost or well-rotted manure to act as a moisture reservoir in dry weather. Maintain the fertility with a mulch of compost each year.

Canes can be planted at any time from OCTOBER until MARCH (1); space them 8–10 feet apart, depending on the vigour of the variety. Immediately after planting cut the canes back to a strong bud 6–9 inches above the soil (2).

As the young canes grow they are spaced out on a framework of wires (3) stretched between posts which should be at least 6 feet high. These young canes crop the following year, so immediately the fruit is picked, cut out the old canes right to the base and tie in the young growths made during the Summer to replace them. Overcrowded growths should be cut out at the base.

Blackberries root easily: just bend down young shoots in JULY, bury the tip in the soil, place a heavy stone on it to weight it down and it will root and be ready for transplanting in OCTOBER (4).

Feed the soil each year with a balanced fertilizer and make sure there is plenty of moisture during periods of dry weather.

PESTS AND DISEASES

Raspberry beetle: (5) the maggots attack the fruits. Spray with derris or malathion as blossom fades and first fruits turn pink.

Cane spot may also prove troublesome; it shows as purple spots on the stems, then the leaves wither. All infected canes must be cut out and burned. Spray with Bordeaux mixture or benomyl at bud burst and again as the blossom fades.

Virus diseases have been identified as infecting blackberries; the canes are stunted and the crop reduced.

RECOMMENDED VARIETIES

'Himalayan Giant' is a vigorous growing, well flavoured berry. 'Bedford Giant' has large well coloured berries. 'Merton Early' ripens mid-season – not too vigorous. 'Oregon Thornless' as the name implies has no thorns but will not succeed in all areas. 'John Innes' is a strong growing, late cropping variety.

Blueberries

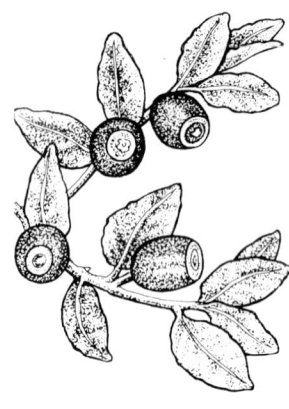

CULTIVATION

The blueberry is a larger version of our native blae or bilberry which grows wild on fellsides and in open woodland. They will only do well in an acid soil, and unlike the bilberry they do need some protection from cold winds. A position in full sun is best, though they will tolerate dappled shade, providing there is no root competition. Oak trees are suitable as top cover: they give some shelter and, because they are deep rooted, there is no competition.

Prepare the site with heavy dressing of peat, leaf mould, rotted manure or compost, but make certain the acidity of the soil is not reduced. Plant the bushes 3 feet apart in early MARCH to mid–APRIL at the same depth at which they were grown in the nursery, then put a thick layer of moisture retaining material on the roots. As the blueberry is not self fertile, plant 2 or 3 different varieties to make sure of a good fruit set. Feeding will not be necessary the first year if the bed has been well prepared. Each subsequent year in MARCH give the plants a dressing of ·complete fertilizer, one specially prepared for rhododendrons will be suitable, at the rate of 2 oz per square yard. An annual mulch of peat or compost will help the soil to stay moist and spongelike.

The fruit forms on shoots grown the previous year, so pruning must be done in such a way as to ensure a constant supply of strong healthy wood. Each year in Autumn cut out a number of old shoots to soil level. This then opens up the way for fresh growth, and ensures a good crop for next year.

Propagation is quite easy. Pull down suitable branches in early APRIL and bury them in a mixture of peat and sharp sand. To keep them firmly embedded, peg them down with a layering pin and put a heavy stone on top of it. This prevents wind rock and conserves moisture as well. Layers are well enough rooted to lift in 12 to 18 months.

Cuttings of half ripened shoots taken with a heel or cut below a leaf joint during the period mid-JULY to the end of AUGUST will root. Trim the heel with a sharp knife, dip the cut in rooting powder and insert in sharp sand.

PESTS AND DISEASES

Birds will gorge on the berries, so it is much safer to net the bushes.

A yellowing of the foliage indicates an excess of lime in the soil. Correct by using acid peat and watering with sequestered iron.

RECOMMENDED VARIETIES

The number of varieties to choose from is limited; the berries are ripe in AUGUST to early SEPTEMBER.

'Jersey' is a regular cropper. 'Bluecrop' grows a large berry, but is not quite so reliable in cropping, particularly if the site is exposed to cold east winds.

CULTIVATION

Acid cherries will only grow well in a free-drainage fertile soil. Prepare the site by deep trenching; at the same time work in a dressing of manure or compost. To make sure the drainage is good, break up the sub-soil with mortar rubble if available.

Acid cherries are usually grafted onto the Malling selection of MAZZARD F12/1 which gives a vigorous, heavy cropping tree.

The trees can be grown fan trained on a wall (1), or as a bush. Yields are better if the soil is kept free of grass and weeds.

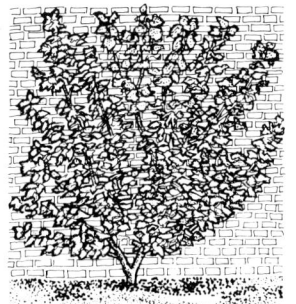

1

In MARCH dress the soil with an all-purpose fertilizer at the rate of 2 oz per square yard. Mulch with rotted manure or compost to ensure the roots are kept suitably moist.

As the trees are self fertile only one need be planted.

Acid cherries fruit on the shoots grown the previous Summer, so pruning must be adjusted so as to encourage a steady supply of new growth each year. Commence pruning in Spring after the buds burst because then growth buds can be easily identified. Space laterals 3 inches apart and cut back some older branches each year to grow strong young fruiting laterals for the following year. PAINT ALL CUTS with protective compound.

Prune and train bush trees to form a balanced framework of branches as growth begins in Spring. Once into crop, prune to keep up a steady supply of 1-year-old shoots which are the heaviest fruit bearers. Cut back the weaker branch ends to good strong laterals growing up and away from the tree.

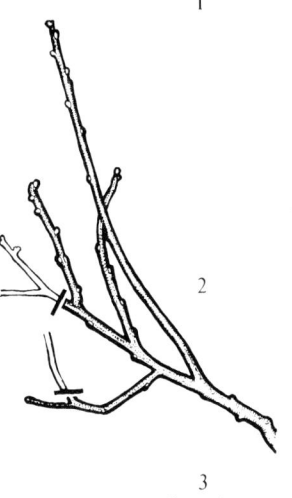

2

Once established, fan trees are trained in the same way: all dead, diseased, unfruitful, overcrowded branches should be removed each year as growth begins (2). This stimulates the growth of young shoots which are then tied in (3) to take their place. PAINT ALL LARGE WOUNDS. PRUNE ONLY IN THE EARLY SPRING.

PESTS AND DISEASES

Silverleaf: a slight paling of the foliage which then develops a grey sheen. The leaves turn yellow and are shed early. When infected branches are cut, they show a brown stain in the wood. Cut all diseased material back to sound wood and burn. Treat with Stockholm tar.

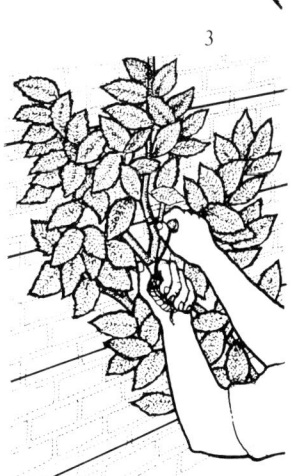

3

Cherry black fly: distorts shoots and leaves. Spray with formothion when the petals fall.

Brown rot: infects fruit damaged by birds. Remove and burn infected fruit. DO NOT PICK FRUIT – CUT STALK WITH SCISSORS. Pulling at the fruit causes damage which increases the risk of brown rot infection.

RECOMMENDED VARIETY

'Morello' will succeed even on a north-facing wall.

Cherries – Sweet

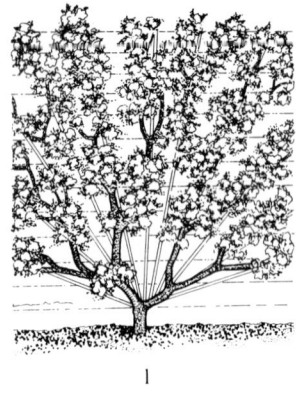

1

CULTIVATION

Because there are no really dwarfing stocks, sweet cherries are frequently grafted onto seedling wild cherries which produce a large tree. Picking the fruit is difficult and the birds eat most of the crop because netting a large tree is a problem. Two trees must be planted as nearly all sweet cherries are unable to pollinate themselves.

When this type of cherry is grown, fan trained, on a wall, allow for 10 feet of spread on each side as a minimum (1). Fan trained trees should have a main framework of branches, spaced 10–12 inches apart and the pruning to achieve this is done in early Spring to cut down the risk of infection from *silverleaf fungus*. Because of this risk, no pruning should be carried out in the preceding Winter.

Shoots growing directly into or out of the wall should be rubbed out as they appear during the course of the Summer. All other shoots, except those needed to fill gaps in the framework, should be pinched back to 4 leaves from the base. Sweet cherries spur up well, so heavy pruning is required only when there are dead or diseased branches to remove, and this should be carried out in late Summer. Pull down strong shoots at branch tips into a tight curve and tie there to discourage further extension growth.

Apply a dressing of complete fertilizer in FEBRUARY and mulch with rotted manure or compost to keep the soil moist in dry weather.

Bush cherries are pruned to form a balanced head, then once cropping begins, cut out the crossing, diseased or dead wood in late Summer. Provided no pruning is done during the Winter, the work can either be done in late Summer or early Spring. While it is easier to train young trees in the Spring, dead or diseased wood is easier to identify on established bush or fan trees in late Summer.

The fruit is allowed to ripen on the tree, then eaten more or less straight away, as it does not store well.

PESTS AND DISEASES

Cherry black fly feed on the young shoots causing distortion. Spray with formothion as buds burst and after the petals fall.

Silver leaf: paling then silvering of foliage. The infected branches die and must be cut off to clean wood, then burned. Treat the cut surface with Stockholm tar. Balanced feeding, watering and pruning ONLY during the growing season will reduce the risk of infection.

Brown rot is a problem if the fruit are damaged in any way (2). Diseased fruits are removed and destroyed to prevent the spread of infection.

2

RECOMMENDED VARIETIES

'Merton Bigarreau', 'Waterloo', 'Governor Wood', 'Bigarreau Napoleon', 'Bradbourne Black'.

CULTIVATION

Blackcurrants grow best in a well drained soil which is kept in a cool moist condition by mulching around the bushes with compost, rotted manure or leaf mould. An open sunny position is the most suitable, but they will produce a creditable crop on a partially shaded site.

Prepare the soil with heavy dressings of compost, manure or any organic waste which will quickly rot down. Blackcurrants thrive on heavy manuring, which maintains a highly fertile soil.

Buy young plants from a nursery which is inspected regularly by the Ministry of Agriculture to ensure that bushes supplied are disease free. Providing the soil has had a month to settle after being dug, planting can be done any time during Autumn and Winter when weather and soil conditions are suitable.

1

Space the bushes 5–6 feet apart and plunge the roots 3 inches deeper in the soil than they were in the nursery (1). This is to make certain branches spring from below ground level which increases their vigour.

All shoots should then be cut back to within an inch of soil level (2).

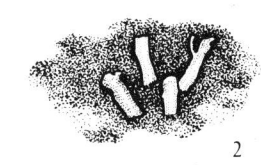

2

This hard pruning stops fruit being developed the first year, concentrating all growth into building up strong young shoots to crop 12 months later. The next Autumn cut out all weak, crossing wood. Pruning of established blackcurrants consists of cutting away one third of the old wood immediately the fruit are picked. All weak, crossing, or diseased shoots are cut out at the same time. Feed the bushes each Spring with nitrogen and mulch heavily with farm manure, compost, spent hops or similar quickly decomposing organic matter. Keep the soil weed free but do not dig near the bushes for they are surface rooted and could suffer serious damage, so only use a hoe or one of the special weed-killing herbicides.

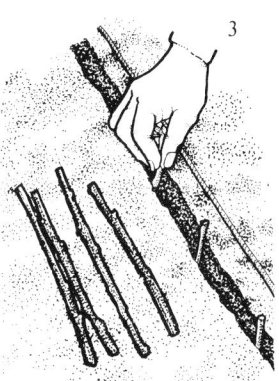

3

Blackcurrants can be propagated fairly easily from cuttings. Shoots 8–12 inches long of the Summer's growth are taken from healthy disease-free bushes. These are inserted in a trench 6 inches deep with a layer of sand in the bottom which the base of the cutting rests in. Only 2 or 3 buds are left showing above the ground level when the trench is filled up and firmed (3).

PESTS AND DISEASES

Big Bud Mite: buds in dormant season are excessively large (4). Hand pick and burn infected buds. Spray with malathion just as the flower trusses develop, repeat the spraying 3 weeks later.

Greenfly (Aphids): young shoots and leaves distorted. Spray with derris or malathion.

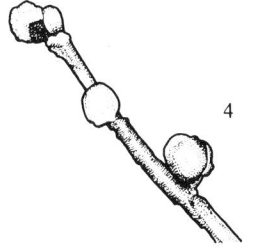

4

RECOMMENDED VARIETIES

'Boskoop Giant', 'Blacksmith', 'Wellington XXX', 'Baldwin'.

Currants – Red and White

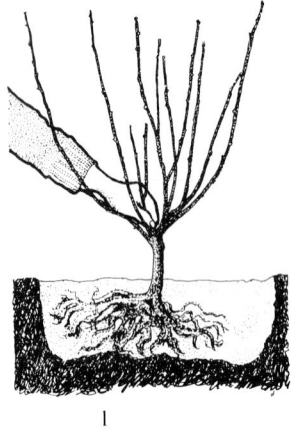

1

CULTIVATION

As with gooseberries these can be grown as bush or cordon, the fruit being developed on spurs and round the base of 1-year-old shoots. Red and white currants will succeed in a rather shaded bed.

Before planting, improve the soil by digging in rotted manure or compost plus a dressing with sulphate of potash, 1 oz per square yard. You can plant at any time during Autumn and Winter when the weather is suitable. Space 5 feet between bush forms, for single cordons 18 inches will be enough. Make certain the roots are well spread out (1). It is best to do the planting when the soil is dry enough to dig easily.

Begin pruning in early JUNE by shortening all side laterals back to 5 leaves. The leaders are left unpruned. In Winter the leaders may be cut back by half to one-third, side laterals to 2 or 3 buds (2). As the bushes get older, worn-out branches have to be removed and new ones trained in to take their place.

Cultivate the soil with annual mulches of rotted farm manure or compost, plus a fertilizer dressing which is high in potash. Both red and white currants need a steady supply of potash.

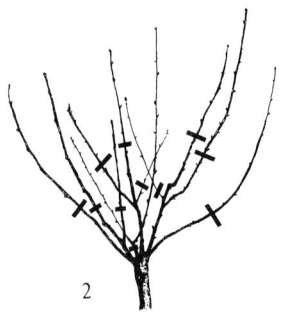

2

Propagation by means of cuttings is fairly easy. Shoots 12 inches long are pushed into sandy compost in OCTOBER (3). When rooted, rub out all but the top 4 buds so there is a clean stem.

The bushes are easier to protect from birds if grown as cordons which take up less space than free growing shrubs. Newly planted cuttings may have the top shoot trained to grow on to form a long main stem. All other shoots should be pruned back to 4 leaves.

Double or triple cordons are formed by cutting back a newly planted well rooted 1-year-old plant hard, then training 2 or 3 strong shoots up to form the stems of the cordon. Tie each shoot to a strong cane as it develops or it may be broken by strong winds.

PESTS AND DISEASES

Birds can strip the ripe fruit in just a few hours, so it is best to net the bushes.

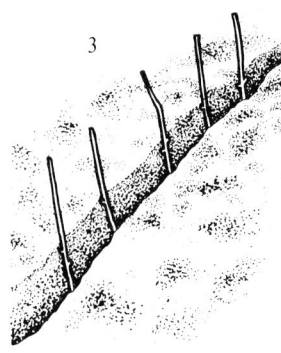

3

Aphids, particularly on bush forms, do disfigure leaves and fruit. Spray with malathion or formothion before, and if necessary immediately after, blossoming.

Coral spot usually first infects dead wood, then penetrates to live tissue. Remove and burn all dead or worn out branches which could serve as a host to the disease.

RECOMMENDED VARIETIES

Red: 'Earliest of Fourlands', 'Laxtons No. 1', 'Red Lake'.

White: 'White Grape'.

Figs

CULTIVATION

Though not widely grown, figs will succeed outdoors in the south when planted against a sunny wall. Further north it is advisable to give them the protection of a greenhouse. The soil which figs are planted into should be well drained, not rich, yet moisture retentive. Figs are grown on their own roots from cuttings or layers. Make a bed 3 feet square lined with paving slabs, brick or concrete (1). Cover the base with lime rubble, old mortar or broken brick hammered down fairly hard. This root restriction is necessary as figs are greedy feeders, making an enormous amount of growth without producing any fruit if allowed to run free. Fill the bed with a mixture of good garden soil – 5 parts soil, 1 part well-rotted manure, and some lump charcoal. The lump charcoal helps to keep the soil from becoming sour when the bed is drenched with water, so encouraging the fruit to swell. Lime in the form of magnesium limestone is usually necessary every third year.

Young pot grown figs can be planted at any time as the root disturbance is minimal, but Spring is the most suitable season as the roots establish quickly. If the roots are pot bound, disentangle and spread them out evenly, working the compost down between them. During the first year space out the shoots as they grow to build up a strong framework. Continue this training for the first few years.

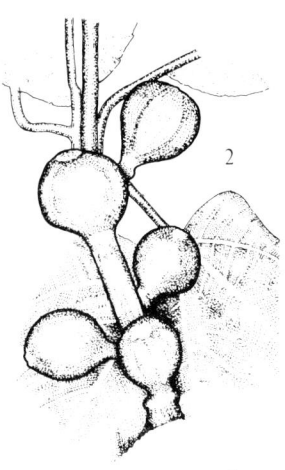

Mulch each year and water heavily as the crop swells. DO NOT over manure or the tree makes all growth and no fruit. Figs fruit in the leaf axils of young shoots (2), so when a tree is old enough to bear a crop, stop side growths at the 4th or 5th leaf before early JULY if possible. This gives the young shoots, which will produce the fruit in JULY/AUGUST next year, time to grow and ripen. Any shoots needed to fill empty spaces are tied in (3), then all surplus growth may be pruned out flush with the parent. This lets light and air circulate freely around the ripening fruit.

The fruit will mature over several weeks, so it is necessary to look at the trees each day. Figs taste their delectable best when allowed to ripen fully, so they are picked and eaten straight from the tree. When ripe there is an obvious change in colour, the base of the fruit cracks and when lifted it parts easily from the twig. In early OCTOBER remove all immature fruits larger than a little finger nail, as these will not mature, except possibly in a heated glass house. The tiny fruit in the tips of young growths will develop to give a crop in the following year.

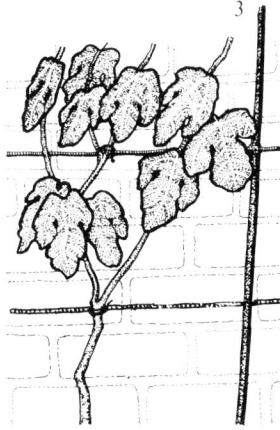

PESTS AND DISEASES

None, apart from die back on pruning snags which may introduce *Coral Spot*. Cut away all snags to healthy wood.

RECOMMENDED VARIETIES

'White Marseilles', 'Brown Turkey'.

Gooseberries

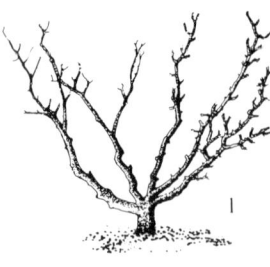

CULTIVATION

Gooseberries are one of the most adaptable fruit grown. They will succeed in most soils and situations, from clay to sandy loam. Though the gooseberry is most often treated as a bush, it can be grown as a cordon, especially useful for producing dessert berries.

Gooseberries prefer a well drained soil, made moisture holding by working in compost, well-rotted manure or leaf mould. The fertility level is kept up by mulching the soil each Spring with the same material.

Young healthy 2- or 3-year-old bushes may be planted up at any time when soil conditions are suitable from Autumn to early Spring. Bushes 4 feet apart – cordon 15–30 inches depending on whether they are single, double or triple. A light dressing of potash will stimulate fruit production. High nitrogen fertilizers which cause soft growth may bring on a heavy attack of the fungus disease *mildew*. Gooseberries fruit on shoots grown the previous season or, in the case of cordons, on short spurs which develop from the main stem. Pruning should be done in Winter to encourage spur formation (1). Cut the leaders back, by half to one-third, always to an upward facing bud. This will build up strong branches. Lateral shoots are cut back to 3 inches. All those which are weak, damaged, or crossing should be cut out flush with the main stem. Any branches growing into the centre of the bush should also be taken out as they may make picking more difficult. To keep the growth neat, in JUNE all lateral growths except branch leaders should be cut to 4 or 5 leaves on bush or cordon gooseberries. This Summer pruning helps to keep the bush open and allows free circulation of air, reducing the risk of *mildew*.

You can begin to pick the berries when they are large enough to cook. This is particularly important when there is a heavy crop as it enables the remainder to swell. Keep the weeds down round the bushes and the ground well mulched with compost. A fertilizer dressing – equal parts nitrogen, phosphate and potash – will help cropping. Cuttings of young shoots 12–15 inches long, taken during the Autumn and pushed into sandy soil, will root (2). A year later they can be transferred to the orchard, after removing all except the top 4 buds to get the bushes onto a clear stem.

PESTS AND DISEASES

Bullfinches disbud the bushes, so put nets on from NOVEMBER to late APRIL. Delay pruning until late Winter.

Sawfly (3): caterpillars defoliate bushes. Spray with derris.

Mildew: spray with benomyl or dinocap.

RECOMMENDED VARIETIES

'Lancer', 'Green Gem', 'Careless', 'Leveller', 'Whinhams Industry'.

Grapes

CULTIVATION

Vines can be grown in a greenhouse with other crops providing these require more or less the same conditions. In a general-purpose house it will be necessary to limit the amount of growth made by the vine, otherwise plants below will be robbed of daylight and air. In a mixed house the vine roots should be outdoors. If the greenhouse is devoted entirely to vine culture, the bed can be made up indoors.

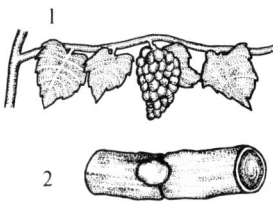

There are terms which occur in grape culture which may need explanation. *Rod* is the main stem. *Spurs* are fruiting side branches developed at intervals along the rod (1). *Eyes* are buds taken on short pieces of stem (2) then rooted in compost.

A bed 4 feet wide by 18 inches deep will be sufficient for one vine. Make up a soil of 3 parts good turfy loam, 1 part sharp sand. This will give good drainage and a top dressing of well-rotted manure or compost, plus 2 oz of bone meal per square yard each year in Spring will hold the moisture. Heavy soils which waterlog do not suit grapes.

A framework of wires spaced 12 inches apart (3) will be needed to support the rod and laterals as they develop. Galvanised or plastic covered wires screwed or bolted to the main roof joists are suitable. These should, of course, be fixed in position before the vine is planted.

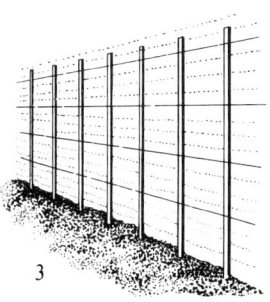

Grapes (continued)

In a greenhouse where other crops are being grown it is frequently found an advantage to have the roots of the vine in a bed outdoors with the rods brought in and trained up the greenhouse in the usual way. The roots being outdoors makes certain the vine enjoys a proper period of dormancy while leaving the maximum space inside for growing other crops, such as ferns, vegetable seedlings and begonia. The bed is made up in exactly the same way as if it were inside.

Growth will start a little later in Spring with newly planted vines. Spray them over daily with clean water, and damp down the border and greenhouse floor to produce a moist growing atmosphere. Remove any flower trusses which appear the first year. The following Autumn cut the rod back by one third. Make certain that growth commences evenly up the stem by letting the end of the rod arch over to restrict sap flow. Water and ventilate as soil and weather dictate.

Tie the leading shoot up to the wires. Laterals are tied in horizontally to train them across the house, and any surplus growths between the wires are removed. The remaining laterals are pinched back to 4 or 5 leaves. Continue to syringe and water through Spring and Summer until the leaves start to change colour in Autumn.

If, instead of training only a single rod, two or three are wanted from each vine, cut the main stem back after the first year to the golden brown, well ripened wood, leaving only one-third of the growth above soil level. As the buds break, select the two or three strongest shoots, taking one to the left, one to the right, and the other straight up. The two outer shoots are turned upwards when they are sufficiently far away from the centre rod, usually 2–3 feet. Any other shoots should be removed and the double or triple rods pruned as for single rod culture.

There are varieties of grapes obtainable which will grow and ripen a crop outdoors. In the more southerly counties grapes are grown for wine making on a field scale. Dessert grapes grown outdoors are best planted on a south-facing wall, so the available sunlight can ripen them to full flavour.

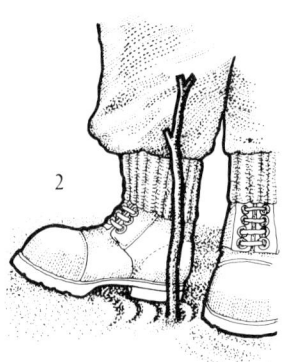

A well drained soil is a necessity so work the planting site to a depth of 18–20 inches (1), mixing in rotted manure or compost. A month before planting the vines dust the soil with a complete fertilizer at the rate of 2 oz per square yard. Plant the young vine during the Autumn, work the soil round the fine roots then firm well down with the feet (2) and water in.

Remove the flowers the first year and tip the laterals back to about 10–12 leaves. Once cropping begins, prune as for indoor vines. Stop laterals at 2 leaves past the bunch. Again experiments have proved that the extra foliage carried when spurs are lightly pruned increases the crop, particularly with grapes for wine making.

Water regularly during the growing season. In Spring apply a general fertilizer dressing at the rate of 2 oz per square yard and mulch with compost or rotted manure.

Prunings can be made into hard wood cuttings 6–10 inches long (1) which if rooted in sharp sand will grow into rods over 2 or 3 years.

When growing grapes on wires in rows, the system is very like that adopted for loganberries. Strong posts are fixed in the soil with wires stretched between. The rods must be planted in well prepared soil during OCTOBER or early Spring. Prune back the rod to 2 strong buds – growths from these are pulled down on to the wires, one to the left and the other to the right of the main stem. The second year cut the weaker of the two back to 3 buds; this will produce the fruiting wood for the following year. The unpruned shoot will carry the current season's fruit. The third year the process is reversed, arranging the pruning so there are fruiting shoots and young shoots growing to replace them the following year.

Established vines: In Spring, when growth commences, select the strongest shoot from each spur and remove all the others. Tie the selected shoots on to wires as they grow. As the flowers open stop syringing the rods and shake the vine at mid-day to help spread the pollen to assist fertilization. As the petals fall start watering and syringing. Ventilate freely when the weather is favourable. Cover openings with netting to protect fruit from birds. Laterals should be pinched back to 2 leaves beyond the bunch of developing grapes.

When the young fruit are pea size take out all the small fruits at the centre of the bunch. Take care not to touch fruit with the hand, as this causes a blemish on them. Use scissors and a small pointed stick (2). A liquid feed after thinning will help to fill the bunches.

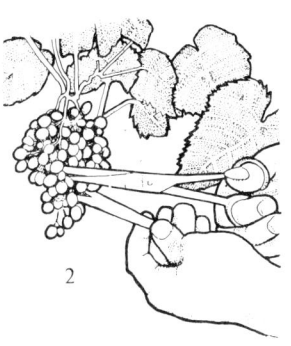

In the Autumn when all the leaves have fallen, remove one-third of the young growth from the lead shoot and cut back the laterals to 2 buds. Though this Autumn pruning may seem severe, it is essential if growth the following year is to be kept under control and in maximum fruit production. A vine allowed to run wild for just one season will produce a large crop of small grapes which because of overcrowded conditions usually rot off with fungus disease.

PESTS AND DISEASES

Powdery mildew: leaves and fruit covered with a white powder. Spray with benomyl or dinocap.

Shanking: stalks of the berries wither. Make sure the growing conditions are correct.

RECOMMENDED VARIETIES

Indoors: 'Black Hamburgh', 'Perle de Czaba', 'Buckland Sweetwater'. 'Muscat of Alexandria' should only be grown in a heated greenhouse.

Outdoors: 'Seigerrebe', 'Seyve Villard 40276', 'Chasselas d'Or'.

For white wine: 'Müller Thurgau', 'Madeleine Sylvaner'.

For red wine: 'Seibel', 'Seyve Villard 18315'.

Loganberries

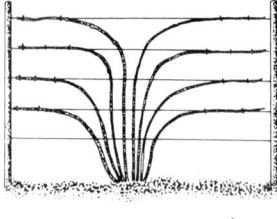

1

2

3

CULTIVATION

Loganberries are not a difficult crop to grow providing the soil is well drained. A good dressing of well-rotted manure provides the moisture which is essential if the berries are to grow fully formed and juicy. Though loganberries will grow in partial shade the fruit has a sweeter, finer flavour when matured in full sun.

The loganberry is invaluable in a small garden because it can be pruned and trained to occupy a small space. Wires are stretched between a framework on a wall or between strong posts 6 feet high in the open garden. Space the wires no more than 12 inches apart so the maximum number of shoots are retained for cropping (1).

Prepare the ground by digging it over 18–20 inches deep. Work in well-rotted manure. Add 1 oz to the square yard of general fertilizer.

Plant the canes (2) at any time from OCTOBER until MARCH, providing soil conditions are suitable, 8–10 feet apart. Prune all top growth hard back to a strong bud 10–14 inches above the soil. As the young shoots grow (see dotted lines on facing page), space them out and tie them in position on the wire for cropping the following year.

Once the canes are established, pruning consists of cutting out old wood after the berries are picked, then tying in a new lot of young canes to replace them. To save the work of disentangling a mass of old and new shoots, keep the young growths loosely in a bundle tied to the most convenient wire. Some different arrangements are shown in the diagram on facing page, (continuous lines show old wood).

Feed established canes in Spring with 2 oz to the square yard of fish meal, then mulch with compost or rotted manure.

Loganberries root readily. At the end of JULY or the beginning of AUGUST bend a young shoot down and bury the tip in a hole 6–8 inches deep filled with a sandy compost. Roots will have developed by NOVEMBER. Cut the cane but do not move the rooted layer to its permanent position until JANUARY. The young cane will produce fruit the second season after planting.

PESTS AND DISEASES

Spur blight: shows as dark purple blotches on the canes. Spray at intervals during the season with captan or theram.

Raspberry beetle (3) maggot feed on the fruit, making them unsightly, spray with derris or malathion at petal fall.

Cane spot: small purplish spots on the cane. Cut out and burn all diseased material. Spray with benomyl as the buds burst, and again after the fruit have set.

RECOMMENDED VARIETIES

'Bauer's Thornless'

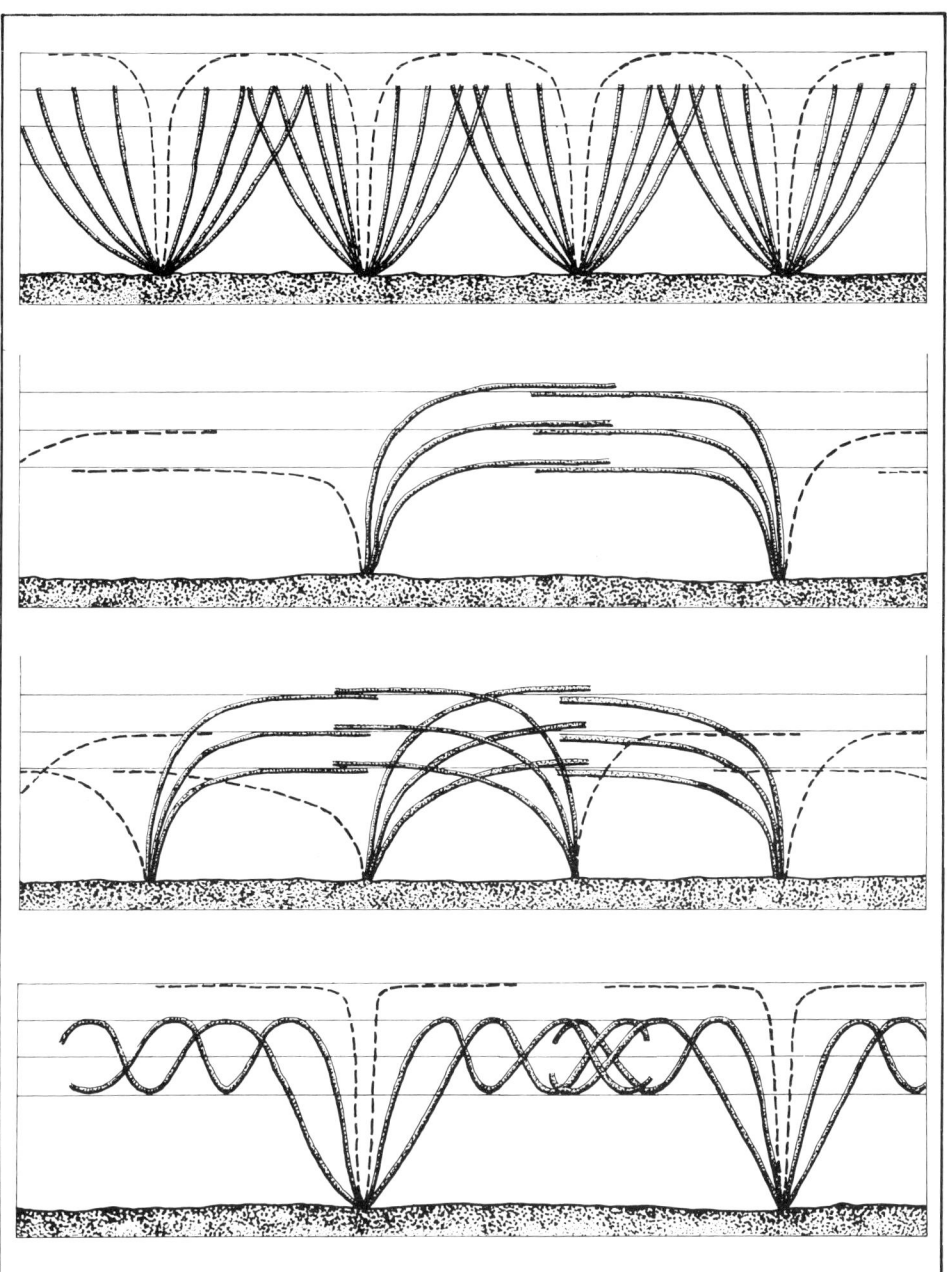

Melons

CULTIVATION

Melons are grown as annuals. Seed sown in Spring will be carrying ripe fruit 5 months later, but they do need protection.

Sow the seed in peat pots filled with compost in MARCH if the greenhouse is heated, otherwise MAY. Place the seeds on their sides ¾ inch deep, water, then cover with newspaper and a sheet of glass. Remove the covering as soon as germination takes place.

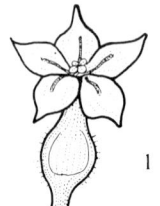

A border in the greenhouse can be prepared by forking in well-rotted manure, then placing 9-inch-high mounds of sterilized loam 18 inches apart into which the seedling melons are planted. Alternatively, they can be grown on in pots or boxes filled with prepared compost. The modern polythene sleeves filled with a special peat-based compost are also suitable for melons.

Train the main stem up canes or wires. When it is about 6 feet high, pinch out the tip to make the side shoots develop; these will in due time produce fruiting sub-shoots. Train the laterals horizontally along the wires. When they are 18 inches long, carrying 4 or 5 leaves, remove tip.

Keep the atmosphere humid by lightly spraying the leaves and floor in hot weather. Ventilate if necessary. When at least 4 female flowers are open (the female has tiny fruit already formed behind the flower (1)), transfer the pollen on to the female flower when in full bloom. Midday in bright sunny weather is best.

Pick the male flower (2) whose stamens are shedding the yellow dusty pollen, remove the petals, then rub the exposed stamens over the female flower (3). Repeat this operation for 2 to 4 days in succession. Pollinate 4 females at the same time to ensure fruit swells evenly. As they swell, stop the shoots one leaf beyond the fruit and start feeding with a balanced liquid fertilizer. When the fruits reach tennis ball size, support them in special nets which can be bought at the local garden store. When fruit is ripening reduce the overhead damping, ventilate on hot days.

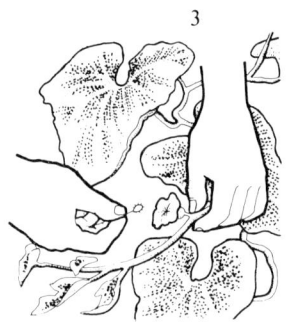

When fully ripe, the fruit has a characteristic fragrance and begins to crack at the base. To check if they are ripe, press the end furthest from the stalk – it should give slightly.

PESTS AND DISEASES

White fly and *red spider:* spray with derris or malathion. Keep atmosphere humid.

Mildew: leaves covered with powder. Spray at intervals with benomyl.

Collar rot: stems turn brown at soil level. Plant on a ridge. Keep water from stem. Dust them with captan.

RECOMMENDED VARIETIES

'Hero of Lockinge', 'Ha-Ogen', 'Honeydew', 'Charentais'.

Mulberries

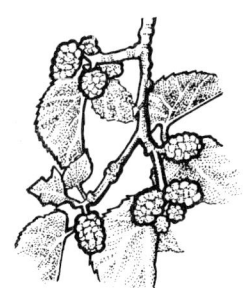

CULTIVATION

A tree can reach 30 feet in height by as much across. Alternatively it can be grown as a dwarf pyramid, or even in a 10-inch pot, but the cropping is irregular when grown in a restricted form.

The fruit looks like a loganberry and is a deep mouth watering carmine when fully ripe. The flavour is not to everyone's taste, so try a few berries before planting a tree. In pies, stewed, or eaten raw, the berries make a welcome change in the menu.

The trees are self fertile, catkins and female flowers being carried on short spurs, so there is no necessity to plant 2 trees. Mulberries are grown on their own roots and are not hard to root from cuttings or layers. To save time, as they do take several years to reach berrying size, buy a 4- or 5-year-old tree from a nurseryman. The variety 'Large Black' grows the best flavoured berries.

A well drained soil which does not dry out in hot weather is preferable. A well grown mulberry is a useful tree for the large lawn, for in addition to supplying the kitchen with succulent fruit, the leaves turn a pleasant soft yellow in the Autumn.

Prepare the site with well-rotted compost, taking care not to damage the roots, which are very brittle, when planting. A stake may be required as a support, but growth is rather slow. Pruning is restricted to removing crossing branches.

When grown as a dwarf pyramid, the single stemmed young tree or maiden is cut back to 20–24 inches. The leading shoots and side growths which break from this the second year are cut back by one-third. Shoots will spring from these and during the Summer this new growth is cut back to 4 leaves and in subsequent years 1 leaf. Growth made above this, continuing the dwarf pyramid, is cut back by one-third the first year and as far as the older branches in subsequent years. When the required height is reached, the topmost branches are pruned as spurs springing direct from the main stem. Ripe fruit is eaten avidly by blackbirds and squirrels. It is impossible to protect large trees, but dwarf pyramids can be netted.

Owners of old established trees may find the main branches need support because the wood is so brittle. Strong wooden posts, their tops padded with a piece of old car tyre, can be used for this.

Allow the fruit to ripen fully on the tree if possible. Gather the crop by spreading a clean sheet under the tree and then shaking the branches vigorously. Fully ripe berries drop on to the sheet.

PESTS AND DISEASES

Very few, other than birds and squirrels attacking the fruit.

RECOMMENDED VARIETY

'Large Black'.

Nectarines

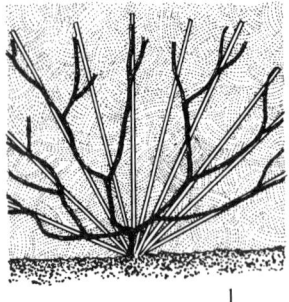

1

CULTIVATION

Nectarines only crop well when grown as fan trained trees against a wall or fence (1). Because the flowers open early in the Spring and are liable to be frosted, the wall or fence gives some protection, and you can put a net over the fan trained trees, whereas it would be difficult with a free growing bush.

Good drainage is important, so when preparing the site break up the soil to a depth of 15–20 inches, working in well-rotted compost or manure. Old mortar rubble or limestone chippings forked into the bottom of the hole will improve the drainage. A position facing due south is best, giving the heat necessary to ripen the fruit to perfection.

DO NOT plant directly at the base of the wall, conditions there may be too dry. Step the roots out about 10–12 inches. Wires stood off from the wall 2 or 3 inches will support the branches of the fan. A gap between the wall and the tree allows the air to circulate. The wall should be cement rendered or well pointed so there are no crevices to harbour pests.

Nectarines are self fertile but as the flowers open when the weather is cold, it is good insurance to go over the bushes with a dry rabbit's tail, piece of cotton wool on the end of a cane or a small camel hair brush to transfer the pollen from flower to flower. About mid-day when the pollen is running freely is the best time. More fruit will set than the tree can carry, so some thinning will be necessary. When the nectarines are the size of a 5-pence piece do the first thinning. Remove all the badly placed fruits and reduce clusters to one. The final thinning at golf ball size should leave the fruit spaced 8–10 inches apart.

As the fruit swell, the tree must be kept moist at the roots or they may split. DO NOT liquid feed unless the leaves show signs of starvation, indicated by poor weak growth and small leaves. Keep the weeds down by push hoeing, not digging, or the roots may be damaged. Alternatively, use a herbicide weed killer.

Fruit is carried on young shoots of the previous year's growth, so pruning is aimed at keeping up an annual supply of strong young shoots to replace old worn-out wood. During the Summer, rub out any shoots growing into or away from the wall and any not required to fill in the framework. A well furnished tree will have fruiting laterals spaced 4–6 inches apart.

Start the replacement pruning in the Spring, when the young shoots are large enough to handle. The difference between the fruit buds and growth buds is obvious. Allow 1 shoot to grow from the base of each shooting lateral. When it is long enough, and still pliable, tie it in loosely to the previous year's shoot which is carrying this year's fruitcrop. This shoot is the replacement when the fruiting lateral is cut out in the Autumn. Growths on fruiting shoots are pinched back to 2 leaves. Remove all surplus shoots which overcrowd the fan and shade the fruit.

Once the fruit is picked, cut out the old shoots to a point just above the replacement lateral. The cut should be made so that there is no snag left to cause die-back. The young shoots can then be tied in to fill the vacant space. Remove all overcrowded, dead or diseased wood at the same time (1). Paint all wounds with protective compound – Stockholm tar.

When picking nectarines handle them with extreme care. Hold the fruit in the heel of the hand, pressing lightly with the fingers near the stalk: when fully ripe it will part easily from the lateral.

Check the tree every day, as in hot weather the fruit ripen very quickly and drop.

Bush trees need much less training once the branches have been spaced to give a balanced head. Cut out overcrowded, crossing or diseased branches. Selected branches which have fruited are cut hard back, so that young healthy flowering wood will grow to continue bearing fruit. Pruning should not be too heavy as this causes a lot of soft, weak growth and a poor crop.

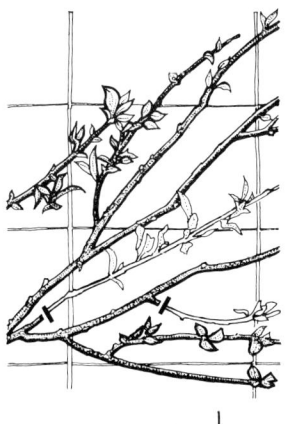

1

PESTS AND DISEASES

Greenfly feed on growing tips of young shoots in Spring. Treat by spraying with a Winter wash in DECEMBER. A spray of malathion or formothion immediately after blossoming will also help to control the pest.

Red spider: the leaves show mottling then turn brown before falling early. Damp down with water during the growing season until the fruit starts to ripen. Treat by spraying with derris or malathion.

Birds and grey squirrels will cause serious damage to buds and ripening fruit. Protect greenhouse doors and ventilators with netting; outdoors net the bushes. With grey squirrels, shooting is the only real cure.

Peach leaf curl shows as large red blisters on the leaves (2). Hand pick and burn all infected leaves. Spray with Bordeaux mixture in FEBRUARY and mid-MARCH, and again in Autumn as soon as the leaves have fallen.

Silver leaf shows as a silvering of the leaves. The infected branches wither and unless these are cut back to healthy wood the tree will die. Do the pruning in Spring or late Summer; paint all large wounds.

Bacterial canker: splitting of the bark which leaks a gum-like substance. Remove all the infected wood and burn. Treat the wounds with a proprietary canker paint. A spray with Bordeaux mixture will also help.

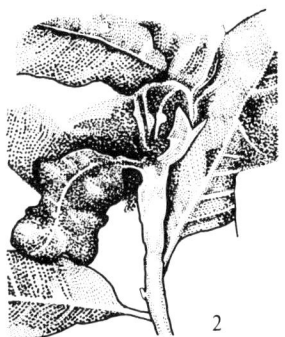

2

RECOMMENDED VARIETIES

'Early Rivers', a good early type. 'Elruge', the most widely planted and hardiest. 'Lord Napier', weak grower but well flavoured, so well worth the effort of growing.

Peaches

CULTIVATION

Peaches are easier to grow outdoors in the colder parts of the British Isles than nectarines. Even so, in the northerly districts the fruit only ripens fully when fan-trained on a wall.

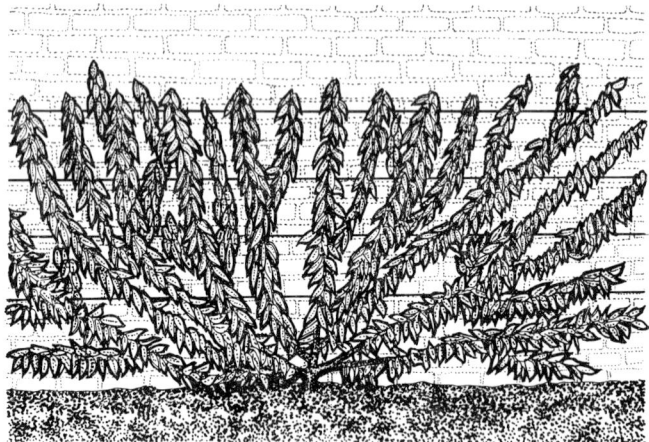

The blossom opens early in Spring and the protection of a wall and netting will prevent frost damage to some extent. Free growing bush trees in the open need less attention to pruning, but it is impossible to protect blossom from frost or fruit from bird damage.

Good drainage is essential, so prepare the site by breaking up the soil 15–20 inches deep, working in limestone chippings or old mortar rubble in the bottom of the trench. The top soil will need enriching with well-rotted manure or compost.

A position facing south or west is to be preferred. When planting fan trained trees on a wall, wires stretched between wooden battens will step the branches off the wall, allowing air to circulate freely. Keep the root 8–12 inches from the wall footings where the soil is dry. The wall should be sound, well pointed, so there are no crevices to harbour pests like woodlice or red spider.

Peaches are self fertile, so need no cross pollination, but as they flower before many insects are about, using a camel hair brush, touch each flower to transfer the pollen. The most suitable time is between 11 a.m. and 2 p.m. when the pollen is shedding freely.

More fruit will develop than the tree can cope with. Remove some of the surplus when the young fruits are pea size, thin finally at golf ball size to leave the crop spaced 10 inches apart on the laterals.

Keep the tree well watered – a shortage of moisture causes split kernals. Use a push hoe or hand weed to keep the bed clean as digging will damage the roots.

How to prune fan trees: Fruit is carried on young shoots of the previous year's growth, so all pruning should aim at keeping up a good annual crop of healthy laterals. During Spring and Summer, rub out all badly placed shoots – those growing into or out of the wall. Remove surplus growths, leaving one strong shoot to every 4–6 inches (1). Leave one bud at the base of a fruiting lateral to tie in as a replacement when the main pruning is completed in Autumn. The terminal bud is pinched back hard to 4 or 5 leaves.

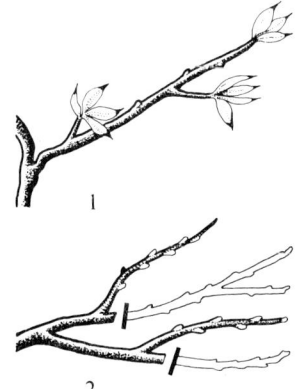

Once the crop is picked, cut out the old laterals (2) and tie in the replacement. Cut all dead, diseased or overcrowded wood clean away at the base. All wounds should be painted with a protective compound like Stockholm tar.

How to prune bush trees: Once the branch framework is set, each branch should be spaced so as to form a balanced head. Bush trees need pruning regularly. Cut out crossing branches, dead or diseased wood. Selected branches may also be cut back hard so that young healthy flowering wood will grow to keep the tree in cropping.

HANDLE THE FRUIT WITH CARE.

A ripe peach gently lifted with the palm of the hand drops easily from the stalk. Check the fruit in the morning and evening as they ripen rapidly in hot sunshine.

PESTS AND DISEASES

Greenfly (aphids) attack young shoots. Spray with tar oil in JANUARY, malathion after flowering.

Red spider: silvery mottling of leaves. Damp down trees morning and evening. Repeat spraying with malathion.

Peach leaf curl: this shows as large red blisters on the leaf. Hand pick infected leaves and burn. Spray with 3% lime sulphur in FEBRUARY –MARCH, and repeat 14 days later. A further spray with lime sulphur or Bordeaux mixture in the Autumn should help to control the infection.

Chlorosis: leaves turn a pale silvery green; fruit reduced in quantity and quality. Usually caused by unsuitable soil conditions. Dress the soil with farm manure and compost. Spray with sequestrene iron.

Silver leaf: this shows as a brown stain in the wood; leaves wilt and die. Cut out and burn infected branches.

RECOMMENDED VARIETIES

'Peregrine' is a good variety for under glass or in the open.

'Dymond' crops well in a greenhouse.

'Bellegarde' is reliably hardy.

'Rochester', hardiest for outdoor cultivation.

Pears

CULTIVATION

Pears need more shelter than apples because they flower earlier and are liable to be caught by Spring frost. In northern areas, to achieve full flavour, pears should be grown, trained ona wall as fans or espalier.

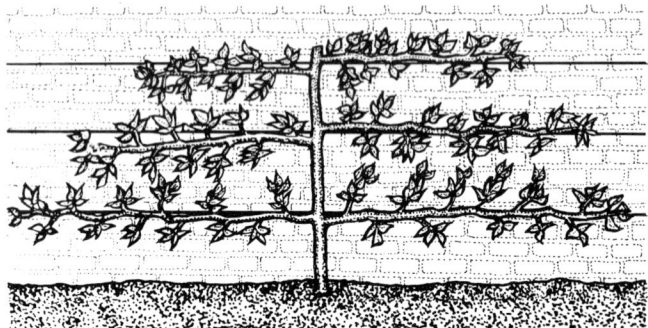

To produce trees which come into crop at an early age, varieties are grafted on to one of the Malling Quince rootstocks. Malling Quince C will give an easily managed tree, not too vigorous, which is the earliest to reach cropping size. Pear varieties grafted on Quince A make rather more growth and take a year or possibly two longer before they reach the fruiting stage. Quince A is the most popular of rootstocks.

Though few amateurs will be interested enough to attempt grafting pears, it should be made clear that not all varieties will join to a Quince rootstock, so the 'do it yourself' man will have to be selective. Another factor which influences the choice of varieties to grow is that almost all pears are self sterile, so to set a crop of fruit two or more varieties must be planted together.

Because pears prefer a deep, moisture retentive soil, the site for them should be prepared with the same thoroughness as for apples. Dig in well-rotted manure, compost or similar organic matter, mixing it well with the soil. This high state of fertility can be kept up after the trees are planted with annual top dressings of manure or compost. In addition to the mulch, an annual fertilizer dressing can be given each FEBRUARY of fish meal at $1\frac{1}{2}$ oz per square yard. This should be enough to provide healthy but not over luxuriant growth, as pears need rather more nitrogen than apples.

Pruning: During the formative years the pruning should be done so as to shape a strong, well spaced framework of branches. This initial training may occupy the first 4–5 years after planting. By the third year strong laterals should be growing from the main branches. Select those which are well placed to help complete the branch framework; these are cut back by one-third in FEBRUARY to an outward facing bud, so should be the leaders on the other branches already established. All laterals should be spurred back to within 3 buds of the base.

Pears (continued)

As with apples, very few pear varieties are tip bearers (producing fruit at the tips of 1-year-old shoots). They are pruned in the same way as tip bearing apples. Because of their upright habit, as the trees mature branches which cross over and overcrowded the centre of the tree need pruning out to let in more light.

There is a tendency with some pear varieties to over-develop spurs, and from time to time these should be thinned down or the quality of the fruit will deteriorate. By thinning out and shortening back, then pruning the shoots which grow from the spurs back to 1 leaf the following Summer, a continuous supply of young healthy fruiting wood will be maintained.

Pears grown on espalier are usually purchased with the 2 or 3 tiers of branches already established. Pruning is the same for both apples and pears. Prune the laterals (young growths of the current season) as they harden up at the base, usually late JULY–AUGUST, depending on the part of the country. Laterals from the main branches are cut back to 3 or 4 leaves from the base. Shoots which grow from spurs instead of direct from the main stem are cut back to 1 leaf only. If the Autumn weather is moist and mild, secondary growth may break from the cut back laterals; cut this back to 1 bud.

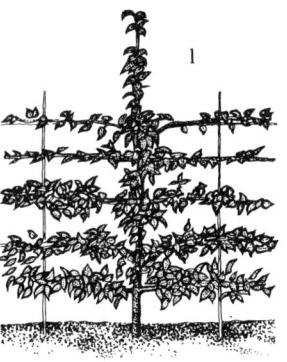

As the spurs age, they may be cut completely away flush with the parent branch. A young lateral can then be pruned to form a new spur as a replacement, if the vigour of the tree warrants. One of the problems with pears and some apples is over-production of spurs, which need regular thinning to maintain a well trained tree (1).

Pears will not crop to full capacity without cross pollination, though it is possible to plant one variety, 'Conference', which is often recommended, and harvest a moderate crop of fruit. As with apples, not all varieties are compatible with each other, so not only will they not set fruit with their own pollen, it is useless for other members of the group. When choosing varieties, consult the nursery who sell the trees and they will advise.

Harvesting: Not all the pears on the same tree will ripen together; with some varieties there may be 10 days difference. When ripe the stalk should break easily from the spur without tearing the wood. With some varieties, particularly the early pears, try the pears for texture, as often they taste best when the flesh is firm and crisp, seemingly unripe.

Late ripening pears, 'Winter Nellis' or 'Packham's Triumph', should be left on the tree till OCTOBER if possible, or the fruit may shrivel in store.

Store the pears, separately, on a shelf or in trays, unwrapped and not touching each other. Pears can be stored in the coolest of conditions without, of course, letting the temperature fall below freezing point. Ripeness for eating is indicated in many cases by only a slight change in colour, so go over the trays inspecting the fruit at regular intervals.

Pears (continued)

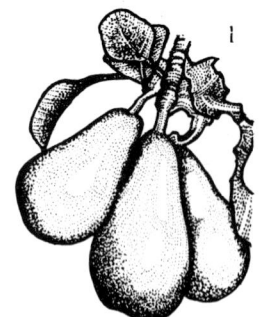

PESTS AND DISEASES

Blister mite causes brown blisters on the leaves in a very heavy attack, and the leaves fall early. Fortunately, this occurs infrequently. In consequence, the wood fails to ripen and dies back at the tips. Hand pick and spray in MAY with lime sulphur.

Birds: they damage the fruit buds in Winter and peck the ripening fruit. Netting or bagging the fruit is the best solution.

Greenfly (aphids) feed on the young shoots which are stunted or distorted. Spray with a Winter wash in DECEMBER to JANUARY, or derris, malathion or formothion just before blossoming.

Pear midge: small maggots feed on the young developing fruit which fall early. Hand pick and burn obviously infected fruitlets. Watering the soil under the tree with tar oil will reduce the number of overwintering insects.

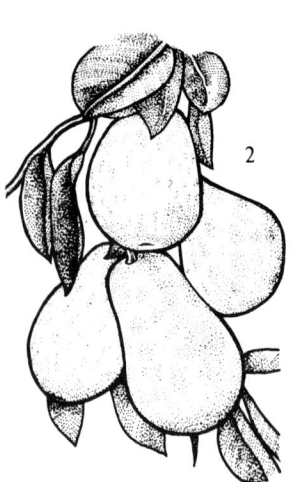

Slugworm: leaves eaten by small black caterpillars. Spray with derris or malathion at the first sign of damage.

Apple capsid: distorts and damages young fruit, which become pitted. Spray with malathion before and after flowering.

Codling moth: tunnels into and spoils the developing fruit. Bands of corrugated cardboard tied round the tree trunk provide hibernation places for the caterpillars, which are then removed and destroyed. A spray with derris or malathion during JUNE will kill the caterpillars.

Brown rot: brown circles on fruit which quickly rot. Remove and burn all infected fruit.

Scab: olive brown spots on leaves, cracks on developing fruit. Spray with benomyl or thiram as the flower buds show, again as the petals fall, then 3 weeks later.

Pear canker: peeling bark on young twigs, die back on branches. Cut out infected wood and burn. Paint all wounds with canker paint.

RECOMMENDED VARIETIES

'Conference' (1) is a reliable pear, a good pollinator, and crops well.

'William Bon Chretien' (2) is a full flavoured variety for cooking or dessert, and can also be relied on to succeed in northern gardens.

'Doyenne du Comice' (3) has such a good flavour it is worth a place in the most sheltered part of the garden, preferably a wall. Spasmodic in cropping and unless sprayed regularly is subject to scab.

'Louise Bonne of Jersey' is reliable in most areas and crops regularly with good quality fruit. Will not pollinate with 'Williams' as the trees are incompatible.

'Packham's Triumph' will keep, with care, until DECEMBER.

'Winter Nellis' is a small pear which keeps well and is suitable as a cross pollinator for 'Conference'.

Plums

CULTIVATION

Plums are usually grown as bush, fan trained, or pyramid trained trees. They will succeed in most soils providing they are well drained, but because they flower early, need a position sheltered from the Spring frosts. Some plums and greengages will set a full crop of fruit with their own pollen. Others need cross pollination, so be careful when making a selection.

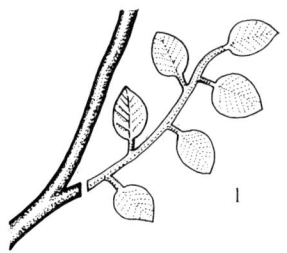

Plant the trees in OCTOBER to NOVEMBER. Newly planted trees require a constant water supply, so mulch with well-rotted compost each Spring, plus a dressing of fish meal at 2 oz per square yard.

Bush trees take up a lot of space unless planted on a less vigorous root stock such as St. Julian A. The Brompton stock is suitable for grafting all varieties but produces a large tree.

DO NOT DIG NEAR THE ROOTS as this can cause suckers to grow from damaged roots. If suckers do grow, pull them away close to the root rather than cutting them.

Pruning: Plums fruit on both young and old wood, so once the tree is mature pruning consists largely of cutting out dead, diseased, crossing or worn out branches (1). Young healthy shoots are then trained in to fill the empty spaces.

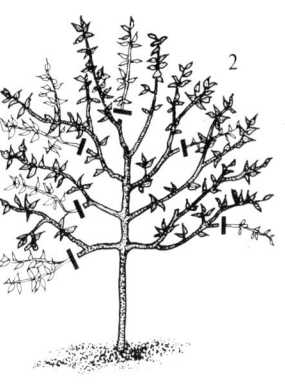

Do all pruning in the growing season: between JUNE and AUGUST. This lessens the risk of infection from silver leaf fungus. Seal all large wounds with Stockholm tar.

One problem which occurs frequently in bush and standard plums is that the centre of the tree becomes a tangle of growth; this should be thinned out when pruning in late Summer (2).

Both plums and damsons can yield enormous crops of fruit when the flowers are not killed by frost. The branches can break under the weight, so support the trees when heavy with fruit (3).

PESTS AND DISEASES

Greenfly (aphids) causes the young leaves to curl up and distort the shoots. Spray with formothion before and after the flowers appear.

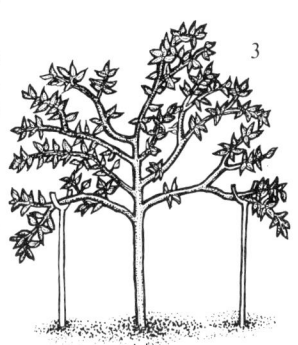

Silver leaf fungus: leaves take on a silver sheen, then twigs and even branches die back. Cut out infected branches to sound, healthy wood. Paint all wounds with a protective compound. Make sure trees are growing strongly by applying a complete fertilizer dressing.

RECOMMENDED VARIETIES

Dessert: 'Early Transparent Gage', 'Denniston's Superb', 'Victoria' (all self-fertile).
Culmary: 'Czar', 'Marjorie's Seedling' ('Czar' is not self-fertile).
Damsons: 'Merryweather', 'Bradleys', 'Prune' (all self-fertile).

Raspberries

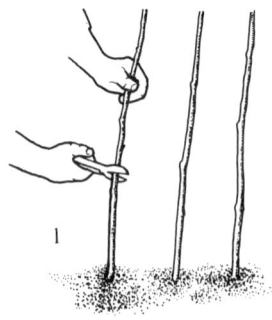

CULTIVATION

Raspberries will crop well in partial shade which, in a small garden, where space is limited, can be an advantage. Always use vigorous, disease free plants, as virus infected material never gives a worthwhile crop. Dig the soil over in late Summer mixing in well-rotted manure, compost or similar moisture holding organic matter. This is important if the soil is at all light, for raspberries are deep rooting and will not crop in poor land. A mulch of manure or compost each year will maintain the soil in a fertile condition. A dressing of high potash fertilizer, at 2 oz per square yard, should be dusted on the soil each year in MARCH.

Plant the canes up in Winter, from NOVEMBER onwards to the end of MARCH. Allow 15 inches between the plants in rows 6 feet apart.

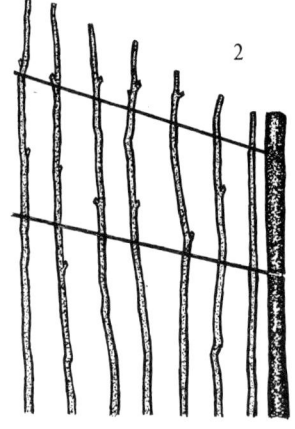

Cut all the top growth hard back to 6 inches above soil level, as it is best not to allow them to carry fruit the first Summer (1). Aim at establishing strong young rods which are tied on to wires stretched down rows of well anchored supporting posts (2).

DO NOT dig the soil too close to the rows as this is the area where the young canes to carry next year's berries will grow from. Only the shallowest of cultivations should be carried out. As a result the young canes will be later starting into growth and will not be fully ripened by the Autumn, when they will be killed by the first frost and have to be cut away. Immediately the fruit is picked, old canes are cut out close to the soil and young canes are tied in to take their place. Five canes per root is usually sufficient, certainly not more than seven; the remainder are pruned away. In late Winter go over the bed shortening back the tips of canes by 3 or 4 inches to a good bud (3).

Autumn fruiting varieties are pruned to ground level in FEBRUARY. Fruit develops in SEPTEMBER on the canes produced in the same season.

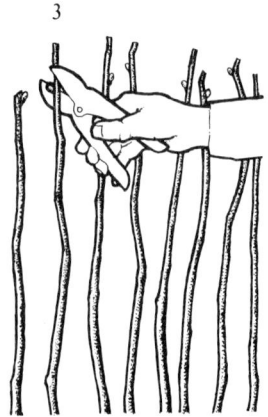

PESTS AND DISEASES

Raspberry beetle grubs feeding on ripening fruit. Dust with derris or fenitrothion as buds turn pink.

Spur blight: leaves wilt and wither. Cut out diseased canes, spray new growth as it develops with Bordeaux mixture or benomyl.

Virus diseases: control greenfly, which may spread disease, by spraying with dimethoate just before blossoming. One of the most common is mosaic yellow spotting of the leaves.

Cane spot damages all the above ground parts, particularly the young stems. Shows as small purple spots on the stems. Spray with lime sulphur at bud burst and again just before flowering.

RECOMMENDED VARIETIES

'Malling Jewel', 'Glen Cora'. 'Malling Admiral' and 'Norfolk Giant'. Autumn fruiting: 'September' and 'Zeva'.

Strawberries

CULTIVATION

Strawberries give the quickest return of any fruit crop, and can be included in a vegetable garden rotation. ALWAYS BUY HEALTHY PLANTS – certified as virus free. Dig the soil a month to 6 weeks before planting, working in plenty of rotted farm manure or compost. A pH test will discover if liming is necessary or not. MAKE CERTAIN there are no perennial weeds like couch grass or ground elder, as these are impossible to eradicate once the bed is planted.

Space the rows 24 inches apart, with 15 inches between the plants, or if the garden is large enough, allow 30 inches between the rows.

Planting can be done from AUGUST to mid-SEPTEMBER, or in Spring, APRIL or MAY. Depth of planting is important and is adjusted so the crown sits just on the soil surface (1). (The crown is the junction between the root and leaves.) Young plants are best de-blossomed to prevent them fruiting the first year if late planted.

In Spring, work a dressing of complete fertilizer down between the rows at 2 oz per square yard. Keep the bed watered in dry weather. As the fruit swells put down straw, polythene or mats to stop the berries becoming soiled. All runners should be removed and, of course, weeds. Netting will be needed in most gardens to protect the fruit from birds and in many gardens squirrels. The simplest method of supporting the net is to make hoops of heavy gauge wire. These can be lined out at intervals. Then, as the fruit swells, the net is stretched over them. Alternatively, short wooden stakes and canes supporting a framework of wire will hold the net well clear of the fruit. Whichever method is used it should enable the net to be removed and replaced with the minimum of effort. After all the fruit is picked, cut off the old leaves, rake them up with the straw and burn them. This clears a lot of pests.

By using cloches to protect the rows the fruit will be ready to pick 3 weeks earlier (2).

Use garden shears to clip over the plants, taking care that the crown clusters of stalks at the centre of the plant are undamaged (3). Remove all the runners so each parent plant is left evenly spaced down the rows. Work along the rows with a hand cultivator, loosening the soil which has been trodden down hard by constant passage of feet during picking, weeding and netting. A dressing of high potash fertilizer can be worked in at the same time.

To propagate new stock outdoors, peg down selected runners into pots filled with compost (4), and plunge them between the rows of the parent plants in JUNE/JULY. By late AUGUST they should be well enough rooted to be cut from the parent and planted out. It is essential not to take runners from diseased plants.

Perpetual strawberries need the same soil preparation as normal crop varieties, but they do not produce such good fruit as the traditional single crop strawberry.

Strawberries (continued)

Ripe strawberries can be enjoyed over a longer season if the selected 1-year-old plants are lifted and potted up for growing in a sun lounge or greenhouse. Runners from healthy stock are pegged down into pots in JUNE. When the pots are full of roots, detach the runners and pot them into 5- or 6-inch pots, using John Innes No. 1 or similar compost which contains sufficient organic fibre. The pots stand outside; feed and water well to build up the strong healthy plants for cropping the following Spring. In JANUARY move the pots indoors, keep them on shelves close to the glass, syringe over and water as necessary. DO NOT try to quicken growth with high temperatures (50°F increasing to 60°F when the flowers open is sufficient). Fertilize the flowers with a camel hair brush or dry cotton wool, or the fruit may be misshapen. As the fruit swells, give a dilute liquid feed every 10 days and syringe over to keep a humid atmosphere. Ventilate freely to reduce the risk of disease. Once the crop is picked burn the plants.

Plants grown under cloches will continue the succession of ripe fruit. Again plant 1-year-old runners, spacing them 10 inches apart. Cover the rows with glass or polythene in FEBRUARY or early MARCH. Open the ventilators. Polythene tunnels should have the side away from the prevailing wind rolled up when the flowers open, to enable the pollinating insects to work. The fresher and more buoyant the atmosphere, the better the crop.

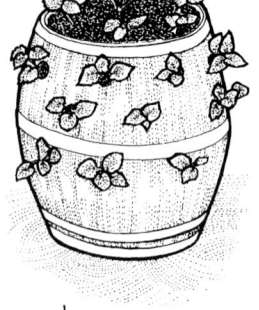

Strawberries can be grown in barrels. Buy the barrels with the holes already made, spaced about 8 inches apart. Place 2 inches of gravel in the bottom to provide drainage, then a layer of leaves about 1 inch thick. The remaining space is made up with a compost of: 3 parts loam, 1 part rotted manure or garden compost, and 1 part sand, plus a dessertspoonful of fish meal to every bucketful of the mixture. As the compost reaches the level of each hole, plant 1-year-old strawberry runners – spread the roots out evenly and firmly. Continue until the barrel is full and every hole is planted (1). The top may also be planted, spacing at 10-inch intervals. Keep the soil in the barrel moist, and liquid feed as the berries set. Pyramids of drain pipes, motor tyres cut in half, anything which will hold compost in large amounts will grow good quality strawberries.

PESTS AND DISEASES

Grey mould (2) causes fruit to rot. Spray with benomyl.

Virus: plants stunted, leaves yellow. Dig up and burn infected plants.

Mildew: fruit goes dull, leaves curl up, turning purple. Spray with benomyl. Burn infected foliage.

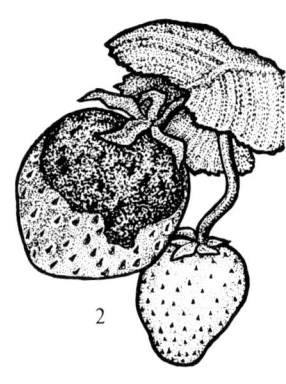

RECOMMENDED VARIETIES

Single crop: 'Grandee', 'Royal Sovereign', 'Cambridge Favourite', 'Tamella', 'Red Gauntlet'.

Perpetual varieties: 'Gento', 'St. Claude', 'Trellisa'.

Monthly calendar of work

JANUARY

Prune apples and pears.

Spray dormant trees with tar oil to control aphis and sucker.

Check stakes to make sure they are firm, and ties that they are sound and not too tight.

FEBRUARY

Providing weather and soil conditions are suitable, plant stock as it arrives from nursery.

Remove tips of Summer fruiting raspberries.

Prune Autumn fruiting varieties to within a few inches of soil level.

Put cloches over strawberries for an early crop.

Complete spraying apples and pears with Winter wash, either tar oil or DNOC petroleum if red spider is a problem.

MARCH

Vines in greenhouses will be starting into growth so spray night and morning with tepid water.

Pollinate peach and nectarines as the flowers open.

Give raspberries and blackberries a dressing of potash fertilizer.

Plant strawberry runners.

Spray apples against scab as buds burst.

Sow seed of melons for early cropping.

Mulch newly planted fruit – blackcurrants, raspberries, etc.

APRIL

Protect early flowering fruit from frost where possible.

Spray peach trees grown outdoors against leaf curl.

Cut back all newly planted raspberry canes.

Spray apples and pears against scab, aphids, etc.

Spray blackcurrants against big bud mite.

Train and pollinate melons as they flower.

Early vines will need training and stopping.

Thin and disbud peaches and nectarines.

MAY

Thin gooseberries when berries are large enough for cooking, taking care to leave the main crop sufficiently spaced to ripen.

Thin laterals on outdoor vines to one per spur: retain those that are showing flower trusses.

Start de-shooting peaches and nectarines outdoors. Leave the main fruit thinning until stones are formed.

De-blossom first year strawberry runners.

Thin unwanted shoots of raspberries – those growing between the rows, etc.

Keep fruit indoors fed and watered.

Stop and train melons – start feeding as fruit swells.

Indoor vines will need bunch thinning, and ventilate as the weather gets warmer.

Repeat the spraying of apples and pears.

JUNE

Put straw or mats down between the strawberries to protect fruit from mud splashes.

Continue picking gooseberries as required.

Pick blackcurrants and raspberries as they ripen.

Thin pears and apples if the crop is heavy before and after the natural fall (June drop).

Cut young shoots on fruiting figs back to 5 leaves.

Pinch out unwanted shoots from fan trained cherries and plums.

Spray raspberries and loganberries against cane spot.

Remove runners from newly planted strawberries.

Melons will be better supported in special nets to take the weight of the fruit from the stems.

Continue to thin grapes as required.

Mulch the beds with rotted manure to conserve moisture.

JULY

Pick strawberries, gooseberries, blackcurrants and raspberries, etc. daily.

Summer prune cherries and plums.

Monthly calendar of work

Keep air on vines under glass to cut down the risk of mildew disease.

Clean up strawberry beds once the crop is cleared.

Peg down strawberry runners to root, remove those which are not needed.

Complete the thinning of apples and pears.

Check plum trees for silver leaf – cut out all diseased branches with the symptomatic silvering of the foliage.

Continue Summer pruning.

AUGUST

Continue to pick fruit as required.

Continue to Summer prune trained forms of apples and pears.

Prune wall trained peaches and nectarines which have fruited.

Prune plums and damsons as the fruit is gathered – remove dead wood and broken branches.

Water, prune or feed vines according to the stage of fruiting.

Prune out old canes which have borne berries from Summer fruiting raspberries.

Prepare soil for planting up strawberry runners early next month.

SEPTEMBER

Pick Autumn fruiting strawberries and raspberries, blackberries, etc.

Tie in the Summer fruiting raspberry canes once the old canes have been removed.

Prune the blackcurrants and take any cuttings required from healthy shoots.

Melons in frames will be ripening so reduce water supply and stand fruit on upturned pots if necessary to keep them clear of the soil.

Put grease bands around the apple tree trunks to trap Winter moths.

Prune loganberries which have fruited.

OCTOBER

Pick apples and pears – store any which are suitable and undamaged.

Take cuttings of gooseberries.

Cloches over the perpetual strawberries will help to extend the season.

Prepare the soil for planting new fruit trees as they arrive from the nursery.

Prune blackberries after all the fruit is picked.

Spray peaches and nectarines against leaf curl.

NOVEMBER

Pick any remaining apples and pears.

Check fruit already in store and keep them well ventilated.

Remove secondary growth from Summer pruned apples and pears.

Make sure all young raspberry canes are firmly tied in to their supports.

Make sure newly planted strawberries are not being lifted by frost.

Once the trees are dormant commence pruning the remaining fruit trees and bushes.

Ventilate freely the vines on the greenhouse once they are finished cropping.

Cut and store any bunches of grapes which are left.

DECEMBER

Inspect fruit in store.

Plant up any bushes and trees as they arrive from nursery.

Check all stakes and ties are sound.

Protect figs planted outdoors.

Start Winter wash spraying of dormant trees.